T McSweeney
author of *English Plus*

On-line English

Achievement in GCSE and how to assess it

with additional material by D. H. Langston

Longman

Longman Group UK Limited,
Longman House, Burnt Mill, Harlow,
Essex CM20 2JE, England
and Associated Companies throughout the world.

First published 1988

Set in 10/12pt Times, Linotron 202
Produced by Longman Group (FE) Ltd
Printed in Hong Kong

ISBN 0 582 00266 4

Scheme of work

Introduction

1 This book is to serve the purpose of the new GCSE Examination in English.

2 The emphasis is on:
   a what you know, understand and can do relating to
   - varieties of writing according to audience and purpose of the writing,
   - reading with discrimination – a wide variety, from the extract to the full text, from the factual to the imaginative,
   - personal reaction to reading material,
   - oral communication;
   b drafting, redrafting and correcting your own writing which leads to self-teaching. The importance of this for continuous assessment assignments is stressed;
   c self assessment;
   d differentiated levels of achievement;
   e a sense of audience and the purpose for which the language is used.

3 The assignments and work set encompass four levels of difficulty which correspond to the seven grades in GCSE. All will be capable of some level of achievement.

4 There are suggested assessment levels and examples of responses throughout:
   a to help the student and teacher recognise the level of achievement;
   b because considering and assessing suggested responses can be another effective way of learning to read with discrimination and of writing in a variety of modes. The objective is the same as conventional methods of writing essays and answering comprehension questions but the means are different.

5 The approach is:
   a to identify the skills involved;
   b to develop and apply these skills;
   c to assess how the skills have been used.

6 To achieve this, the work is organised into:
   a exercises on specific skills;
   b work which covers a limited range of objectives or at the lower level of responses in the GCSE grade range. This will be suitable, therefore, either for the first year of the course or for those who may have difficulty achieving the higher grades;
   c material which assesses a wide range of objectives and gives the opportunity to produce work along the full range of GCSE grades.

Sense of audience

Choose the language to suit your audience and purpose

Register

If you give a talk or tell a story to a group of infants you choose words, length of sentence and manner of speech to suit the children. This is an obvious example of a sense of audience, but the idea behind it is very important in any writing or speaking that you do, because we change the types of words we use and even the types of sentences according to the person we are speaking or writing to.

On formal occasions we use a different type of English to what we use when chatting to friends. To some extent, language is like clothes: we dress up for some occasions and we have casual clothes for other occasions. The appropriate type of language for an occasion is called **Register**.

Practice

1 What type of English, formal or casual (colloquial),
would you expect on the following occasions?

a the television news
b an interview for a job
c an interview on a TV talk show
d phoning for the time of a train

e talking to a very close friend
f a disc jockey's pop programme
g a football commentary
h a letter applying for a job
i a letter to a friend about the job
you have applied for

2 Choose one of the occasions listed in question 1 on page 8 and write it out in the appropriate type of English, i.e. register, and do it again in an inappropriate register.

3 What sort of situation is indicated in each of the following?
  a Dear relatives and friends of the deceased
  b And now over to Wimbledon where the final set has just started
  c Hiya Smithy!
  d Jenny did well in Part A, but had not revised magnetism for Part B.
  e If my Right Honourable friend would keep his mouth shut, he might hear something.
  f Visitors are requested not to be noisy.
  g Look, man, shut it.
  h Look, buddy boy, shut it.

4 What difference is there between
  a It is quite correct.   **b** She was lovely to look at.
    It's OK.   She was beautiful to behold?

Formal English for formal occasions.

**Long or
short words?**

The practice exercises on pages 8 and 9 point out the difference between
formal and informal English. Although there are no hard and fast rules as to
what makes English formal or informal, the following are some general tendencies

1 Shortened words tend to create a less formal effect than the full word.

exam	examination	TV	television	phone	telephone
lab	laboratory	Maggie	Margaret		
brill	brilliant	Joe	Joseph		

It sometimes happens that the shortened version becomes the normal word and
the full word then sounds rather pompous or old fashioned.

taxi   taxi-cab   bus   omnibus

What effect are newspapers trying to achieve when they refer to the royal
family as Andy, Di, Charlie? How is the Queen generally referred to in
newspapers?

2 If there is a long word and a short word with the same meaning, then the long
word tends to sound more formal than the short word.

commencement	start	incarcerated	in prison	inebriated	drunk
proceed	walk	purchase	buy		

3 Sometimes groups of words are used when one word or a shorter expression
would give the same meaning. Such groups of words sound formal or even
pompous. They are sometimes used deliberately to poke fun at people who are
putting on airs, e.g.

rodent operator   rat catcher   refuse disposal agent   dustbin man

4 If you use too many long words when short words are available then you run
the risk of sounding pompous.

Practice

1 Look at the following notice outside an Exam room. Re-write it in simple
English without changing the meaning.

Before the commencement of the examination all participating students
whether male or female must ensure that all receptacles for books etc. are
deposited outside the examination room.

2 Write out the two following sentences in a more direct form.
   a An attempt will be made by us, as of now, to try to achieve an agreement.
   b It may be possible that you might be desirous of purchasing an item which
      exceeds and surpasses the amount of available money at your disposal.

3 Look at the example above of rodent operator and think up similar types of
descriptions for:
a teacher   an office cleaner   a bus driver   a window cleaner

Read over what you have written and correct errors.

Informal English

There are different degrees of informal English, i.e. colloquial and slang.

Colloquial English

Colloquial English is the less formal type of English we use in speech. Although the colloquial forms of English nearly always start in speech, many have found their way into the written language and give an informal flavour to your writing, e.g.

It's it is
he's **won't** **didn't**

These are shortened forms which are very common in speech, even in formal speech. When they appear in writing (except, that is, in written dialogue) they produce a slightly informal effect and therefore should not be used in strictly formal situations, e.g. an application for a job.

Many words can take on a colloquial tone in certain circumstances, e.g. 'Look here, **old boy**'.

Old and **boy** are normal words but in the context they form a colloquial expression.

Practice

1 Consider the following expressions. Are they similar to the expression old boy?
young man   old girl   old woman

2 What is the difference between the underlined word in the following:
  a a <u>rotten</u> banana   <u>rotten</u> luck
  b <u>dead</u> cold   cold <u>dead</u>
  c The weather's <u>lousy</u>.   The child's head was <u>lousy</u>?

Be clear – be precise – be accurate.

Clichés

A cliché is a stale or worn out expression which has been used so often that it no longer has its full original force. Most people use them in speech but they should be avoided in formal English, particularly if they are a substitute for thinking.

The advice 'Avoid clichés like the plague' contains a cliché itself. Other examples include:

to give him a taste of his own medicine   over the moon
a storm of protest   sick as a parrot
dead as a door nail

Slang

Slang is colloquial English taken one step further away from formal English. It should be used only in dialogue or when you are trying to achieve a particular effect. Even then the following need noting:

1 Slang is often the language of a small group and may not be understood by outsiders, e.g. cockney rhyming slang as in **'trouble and strife'** for wife; **'butcher's hook'** for look.

2 Slang words and expressions can often have a very short life and quickly go out of use.

3 On the other hand, slang words and expressions can eventually become part of normal English, e.g. **mob**, **fuss**, and **rowdy** were once regarded as slang words.

Practice

1 Divide the following words into what you think are formal, colloquial, slang or informal
  a dog   canine   quadruped   mongrel   cur
  b cat   moggie   puss puss   feline quadruped
  c wheels   car   banger   automoblie
  d pal   friend   mate   companion
  e father   dad   daddy   old boy
  f mother   mum   mam   mummy   old girl

2 Try to think of other groups of words which can be treated in a similar way.

Between you and I, this is wrong.

Formal English

As with informal English, formal English should be reserved for appropriate occasions. The effect of using formal English on inappropriate occasions should be noted.

Technical language

All topics have words and expressions which refer to special aspects of the topic, e.g.

cranium   hydrogen   graph   gear box

If your audience is a general one, you will probably have to explain those technical terms which are not generally known; otherwise they will not understand you. Read the following passage taken from a book which was intended to explain to non-scientists the way science affects our every day life. Which terms in it need explaining before you can understand it?

HOW DOES HAIRSPRAY WORK?

Hair sprays are solutions of a plastic in a quick-drying solvent; they cover the hair with a plastic film strong enough to hold the hair in place. The first hair sprays often used shellac, but a wide variety of plastic resins and solvents are now used to provide easier application and better films.

A common plastic used in hair sprays is PVP (polyvinylpyrrolidone). It is often blended with a plasticizer, to make the plastic more pliable and 'bouncy', and a solvent-propellent mixture. Silicone oils are sometimes added to give the hair a sheen. Since PVP tends to pick up moisture in damp weather, another plastic, vinyl acetate, is sometimes added to provide an 'all-weather' hair spray.

Practice

Technical words cannot be avoided but you need to decide which words need explaining. Consider the following subjects and make a list of the technical words necessary for explaining the topic to a listener. Which of the words would you expect the listener to know already?

1 Computer studies – soft-ware, hard-ware, input, user-friendly

2 Baking a cake

3 Basic first aid

4 Changing a plug on an electrical appliance

5 Explaining the working of a car or motorcycle

6 Describing a music centre

Note the following   Jargon is a form of technical language which excludes the listeners. Technical words are often long or sound learned, and as such they appear to have a very formal effect.

Have you covered the topic as fully as possible in the time?

Mankind is your audience

Many people now accept that the English language is not fair to women. There are many occasions when speaking about or to both men and women, we use a word referring only to men. The heading of this section is one example. Another is such a simple sentence as:

Anyone who has ever lost his keys will understand.

Although some people are not bothered by this, if it gives offence it is better avoided. The following are some general guidelines.

1 To use **he or she, his or hers** once may be acceptable, but repetition will sound clumsy.

2 As **they** and **them** can be masculine or feminine, try to use the plural, e.g.

The average reader knows what he likes.
Most readers know what they like.

3 **Ms** for the feminine equivalent of **Mr** is becoming increasingly common.

4 If it is obvious that the statement refers only to a man or woman, then use the appropriate words, e.g.

Anyone in this men's club is entitled to his opinion.
Anyone on the women's committeee is entitled to her opinion.
Actress wanted for the main part in *Heidi*.

5 The feminine forms of many words no longer need to be used and should be avoided as they seem condescending, e.g.

author   poet   sculptor

6 On the other hand, the femine form of some occupations where they used to be mainly men, but now there are many women, is commonly used, e.g.

policewoman   postwoman   milkwoman

7 Avoid obvious contradictions, e.g.

Betty is a dustman.

8 Avoid statements which could be misleading, e.g.

Every single pupil was in his place.

If this refers only to a boys' class then it is acceptable. If it refers to a mixed class and is meant to refer only to the boys in it, then it is still acceptable. Otherwise it is misleading.

9 Do not assume that some occupations are always male and some always female, as in:

A doctor who mumbles to his nurse will find that she does not understand him.

Words state, but also imply.

10 Try to find words which apply equally to women as to men, e.g.

steward/stewardess – flight attendant or cabin crew
spaceman – astronaut
foreman – supervisor

Practice

1 Which word would you use in the following sentences? If you are dissatisfied with the result, rewrite the sentence.
   a The robber got away in his/her car.
   b He/she who hesitates is lost.
   c Anyone found guilty of child abuse deserves to lose his/her freedom.

2 Comment on the following:
   a Mankind is your audience.
   b She applied for a job as a fireman.
   c I do not speak only to the people of my own country, I speak to all men all over the world.
   d The shop was easily robbed because it was manned by only two women.

Language to impress

People often use technical or learned sounding words in order to impress their audience. This can be taken too far so that the result is they can sound pompous. The following is an amusing way of showing how easy it is to sound impressive without really saying anything. It was originally devised by a Canadian Government Department.

1 integrated	1 management	1 options
2 overall	2 organisational	2 flexibility
3 systematised	3 monitor	3 capability
4 parallel	4 reciprocal	4 mobility
5 functional	5 digital	5 programming
6 responsive	6 logistical	6 concept
7 optimal	7 transitional	7 timephase
8 syncronised	8 incremental	8 projection
9 compatible	9 third generation	9 hardware
0 balanced	0 policy	0 contingency

All you need to do is to take any three-digit number and put these words together to get an impressive sounding phrase which means very little. e.g.

2. 4. 2. = overall reciprocal flexibility
0. 5. 7. = balanced digital timephase

Use a dictionary to check spelling.

The reading age of written material

This section began by considering how we use a different type of language (words, sentence structure, tone of voice) when we talk to infants. This introduced the idea of a sense of audience. In order to develop a sense of audience in your own writing, it can be useful learning how to assess the reading age of a passage, book or newspaper. The following is a description of how this is done.

The reading age of a book or magazine depends on the length of the sentences and the length of the words. People with reading difficulties cannot understand long sentences, and have trouble trying to read long, unusual words. Books with a 'low' reading age, therefore, have short sentences and short words, and books with a 'high' reading age have longer sentences and a higher percentage of long words.

You can use the length of sentences and words to find out the reading age of a book, magazine, instructions (e.g. on a food packet) or official form:

● Choose styles of writing as varied as possible.

● Select three 100-word passages from each piece of writing.

● Count up the number of *syllables* in each passage and find the average (giving an indication of the length of words).

● Count the number of *sentences* in each passage, making an estimate of the fraction left over, and again find the average (showing how long the sentences are).

● Find out where the two figures (for each passage) intersect on the chart. The reading age of the piece of writing can then be read off between six and sixteen years old or college standard.

The college principal is your pal.

Chart for calculating reading age

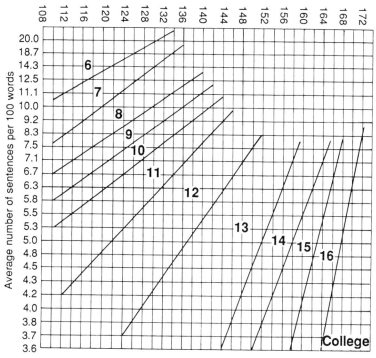

Average number of syllables per 100 words

Here are some results found
by other people:

	Reading age
Articles in *Daily Miror* and *The Sun* newspapers	9-16
Instructions on soup packets	10-17
National Insurance Guide for women	10-17
Claims for industrial injury	10-18
Family allowance for immigrants (in English)	13-18
Highway Code	13+
Income tax form	15-18
Family Income Supplement form	16+
Average trades union form	17

> Practice

1 What general message do you get from the information regarding the reading age of official forms?

2 Look at the extracts on pages 28 and 125 and assess the reading ages needed to read them.

3 Take extracts from a Science book, a Geography book and an English book that you use, and work out the reading ages of them. Comment on their appropriateness for your age group.

Words have meaning and associations.

Letters

Many people dislike writing letters; perhaps they find it difficult and perhaps they are afraid of showing themselves up by making mistakes. This need not be so, particularly if you keep in mind the following:

1 the **person** you are writing to,

2 the **purpose** of the letter and the reason you are writing,

3 the **layout** of the letter.

From this information you should be able to decide whether the letter is formal, informal or semi-formal. When you have decided this you need:

1 the **layout of the address on the envelope**,

2 the appropriate **layout of the letter**,

3 the **correct register**, i.e. you should not use informal English in a formal letter such as a job application; likewise, formal English, particularly the greeting and signing off, sounds odd in an informal letter to a friend.

Practice

Which type of letter (formal, informal or semi-formal) do you think each of the following would be?

1 To a friend after a holiday

2 Inviting a friend to a wedding

3 Applying for a job

4 To a newspaper

5 From a parent to school asking for son/daughter to be excused from P.E.

6 To an aunt thanking her for a birthday present

7 To a firm complaining about a faulty item

8 The first letter to a pen friend

Dear Mrs Smith, – Yours sincerely,

Address on envelope

Whether the letter is formal or informal the address on the envelope is always formal. Why do you think this is so?

Look at the envelopes below:

```
Mr Penter
11 Davis Avenue
BERKHAMSTED
Herts
HP4   2SS
```

```
Mr Penter
11 Davis Avenue
BERKHAMSTED
Herts    HP4   2SS
```

Remember to:

Write the postcode in block capitals.

Do not use punctuation in the postcode.

Leave a clear space between the two parts of the postcode.

Never underline the postcode.

The postcode should always be the last item in an address, preferably on a line by itself.

If it is not possible to put the postcode on a line by itself, it should be placed to the right of the last line of the address. Leave a clear space in front of the postcode.

Layout of letter

The following are examples of general layouts of formal/business letters and informal letters.

Layout and content of informal letter

Note the following:

1 Your address is normally indented.

2 Date.

3 The normal greeting is **Dear**.

4 The normal signing off can take different forms, e.g. **Best wishes**.

5 The content may include colloquialisms or slang according to how well you know the person.

Capital letters for people's names

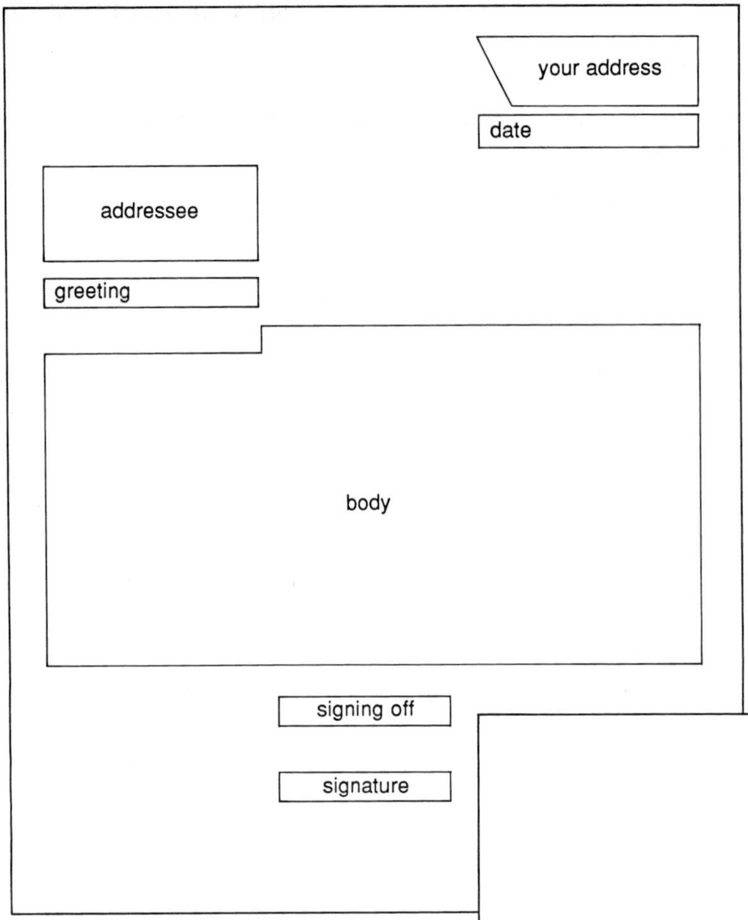

Layout of a business letter

- your address
- date
- addressee
- greeting
- body
- signing off
- signature

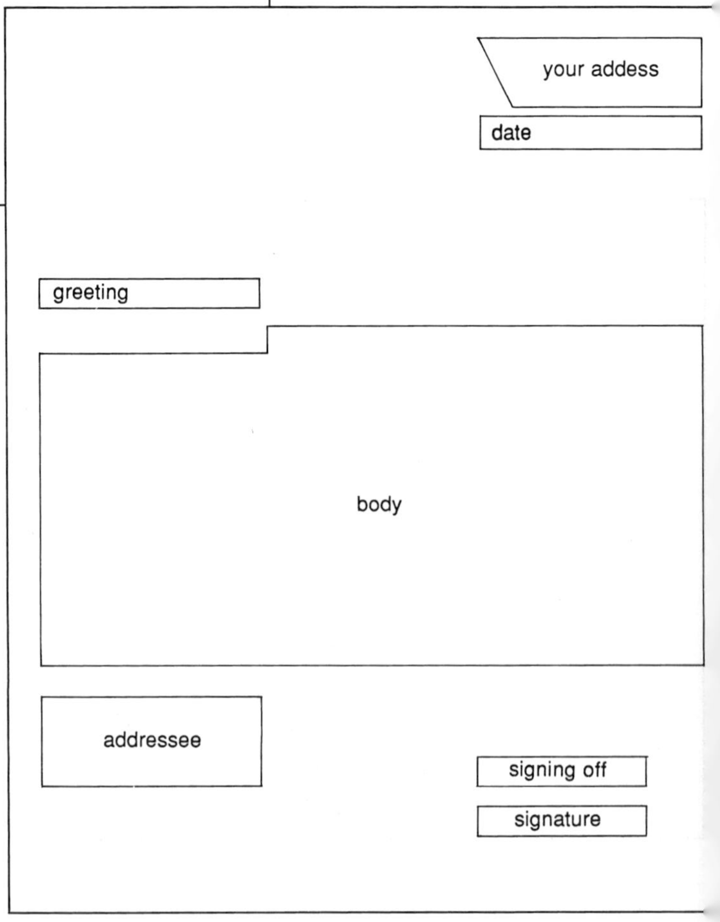

Alternative layout of a business letter

- your addess
- date
- greeting
- body
- addressee
- signing off
- signature

Layout and content of formal letter

Note the following:

1 The general outline is the same as for an informal letter, i.e. with your address indented and the date below.

2 In addition formal letters often have the following:
a **reference number,**
a **heading** stating the subject of the letter,
the **name and address of the person to whom you are sending it**. This may be immediately above the greeting on the lefthand side or after the signing off on the lefthand side.

3 Examples of the **greeting**:
Dear Sir   Dear Madam   Dear Ms Tilly

4 **Signing off**
If the letter begins with **Dear Sir**, **Madam**, **Ms**, the signing off is **Yours faithfully**.
If the letter is addressed to a person by name, i.e. **Dear Mr Smith**, the signing off is **Yours sincerely**.
Note the capital **Y** but small **f** or **s**

5 The **content** should state the purpose of the letter and give any relevant information. The language used should be formal English, but try to avoid the types of English often found in business letters, e.g. I am in receipt of your communication of the 15th ult.

Good practice guide – letter writing

1 Decide whether the letter is formal or informal.

2 Your address and the date in the top right hand corner.

3 In a business letter, put the name and address of the addressee either:

above the greeting; *or*
at the bottom left

4 For formal letters, a formal greeting and signing off.

Dear Sir, . . . Yours faithfully.
Dear Mrs Smith, . . . Yours sincerely,

5 In formal letters, the content should state the purpose, state a case and indicate what needs to be done.

6 Do not use informal English for formal letters.

7 Make certain your signature is legible. If necessary, print your name below your signature.

Dear Sir, – Yours faithfully,

Practice

1 Arrange the following in order of formality.
Dear Smith, Sir, Dear Liz, Betty Dear,
Dear Mrs Smith, Dear Madam Dear Betty, My Dearest Betty

2 Which of the following would go appropriately with the above greetings?
I remain, your obedient servant, Lots of Love,
Yours faithfully, Yours sincerely, Kindest regards,

3 Draft appropriate letters for the following:
a To the BBC or ITV for tickets to take part in a television give-away show.
b Imagine you took part in the show; write a letter to a friend describing what happened.

Overall practice

1 Find shorter ways of expressing the following (the first is done for you):
for the reason that – because
on account of the fact that
subsequent to
in the vicinity of
by virtue of the fact that
adequate bus transportation
a large proportion of
exceeding the speed limit
in view of the fact that
render assistance to
I am of the opinion that
At this point/moment in time

2 Suggest better ways of expressing the following clichés or slang expressions:
beating a hasty retreat
clean pair of heels
cool as a cucumber
leave no stone unturned
explore every avenue
at daggers drawn
the long arm of the law

Do not use informal English in a formal letter.

none the worse for wear
the writing on the wall
at the end of the day
when it comes to the crunch
the name of the game
is what it's all about
in this day and age
to get down to brass tacks

3 Point out the emptiness of the clichés in question 2 (or others that you can think of) in the following ways:
   a combine as many as possible into complete sentences which may sound impressive but say very little, e.g. The name of the game is what it's all about.
   b Use the cliché in a context which is closely associated with the literal meaning of a word in the cliché, e.g.
   As soon as I saw the graffiti all over the new shopping centre, I knew the writing was on the wall for it.

4 Politicians, newspapers and especially the sports sections, are great users of clichés. Compile a list of clichés which you have found in:
   a a selection of newspapers
   b political reports and discussions on the television

5 Draw up columns with the headings **Slang**, **Colloquial**, **Normal**, **Formal**, and place the following expressions in the appropriate columns.
   a browned off   fed up   bored to tears
   b pinch   steal   nick   misappropriate   lift   swipe
   c enjoyable   smashing   dead good   great
   d face   mug   physiognomy   kisser
   e konk   nose   snout   proboscis
   f abdomen   tummy   belly   paunch   stomach
   g lie   fib   untruth   inaccuracy   mendacity
   h guy   feller   man   chap   gentleman   bloke
   i brass   money   cash   dough   lolly
   Point out any which may go into different columns according to the way the are used.

6 Re-write the following in simpler English.
   a Consideration should be given to the possibility of carrying into effect alternatives to the times of inter-city trains.
   b I am of the opinion that if you proceed in the vicinity of that hostelry which is a well-known den of thieves, you will eventually finish up in close proximity to the individual you wish to apprehend.

Fewer in number, less in amount

Reading with discrimination

* Candidates' answers included for assessment

Why do we read?

There are two main reasons: for enjoyment, e.g. novels, and for information, e.g. instructions. These may be quite separate or overlap. When we read for information we generally have to act as a result of it. What type of reading activities are involved in the following?

going shopping
a newspaper
making a cake
going on a long journey by
    different means of transport

a comic paper
a crossword puzzle
an application for a job
magazines

For which of these is there a follow-up, either in writing or action?

Quick reading

Sometimes we need to read quickly and take in only the main points of a passage. You can train yourself to read in this way. With practice you can read short passages and immediately grasp the main facts. Test yourself on the following passages. There are questions on page 34.

Execution Dock

On the banks of the Thames in London near Wapping is a place called Execution Dock. This is where convicted pirates were executed. When the tide was low the condemned man would be staked out just below the high water level. This meant that as the tide came in it would slowly drown him. However a new method of execution, but equally grim, was introduced about the sixteenth century. The pirate was hanged in chains from a high gallows and his body left to rot. This was meant to be a visual reminder to any would-be pirates of the punishment in store for them. Captain Kidd, the famous pirate, was one of them executed in this way.

Cost of trainers

There are four types of trainers advertised. The cheapest one is only £9.95 a pair but they are very plain and have no trade name nor coloured flashes on them. The dearest are £29.95. They are specially designed for high performance, have aerodynamic built up heels and have the latest Addidas flash on them. The trainers with last year's Addidas flash are £5.00 cheaper. There is a new brand called Aerorum which costs £26.50. They have five different colours with a gold trim around the ankle tops. They certainly look different.

Accident

The accident happened at 10.25 a.m. at a cross roads controlled by traffic lights. Visibility was good, for it was a sunny cloudless day. The road surface was slightly damp as there had been a brief shower of rain earlier. It is a very busy road junction with a constant flow of traffic in all directions. A Ford car and a large van were involved. The Ford car was turning right into Fairtree Road from Oak Road. The van was coming in the opposite direction on Oak Road and hit the Ford on the passenger side. Extensive damage was done to the car, but the driver and two passengers escaped serious injury. The van driver had cuts on her face which had hit the windscreen.

Read the passage at least twice.

Assessment guide – reading with discrimination

The following four broad levels of achievement indicate what you are expected to be able to do at each level when reading with discrimination. They are accumulative, that is, to achieve any level higher than the basic you have to be able to do what is indicated at the lower levels.

The four groups are *roughly* equivalent to the GCSE grades as follows:

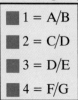

■ 1 = A/B

■ 2 = C/D

■ 3 = D/E

■ 4 = F/G

Use them as a guide

- when looking at your own answers to the reading passages or full text study

- when assessing the answers given to the questions on the reading passages

Level 4
1 Identify broad outlines of passage
2 Note the sequence of events
3 Note general outlines of characters
4 Select fairly obvious material

Level 3
5 Collate information and summarise it
6 Interpret
7 Evaluate in broad terms
8 See different points of view
9 Distinguish between fact and opinion and between figurative and literal use of language.

Level 2
10 Identify writer's technique and explain it
11 Develop ideas in the text
12 Show relationship between parts of the passage and the full passage
13 Reflect on the overall topic

Level 1
14 Identify writer's intentions and comment on them
15 Evaluate, illustrate and comment on ideas in the passage
16 Comment in greater detail on technique

Good practice guide – reading with discrimination

1 Read the passage through without pause.

2 Read it again more slowly noting the way the writer develops the main outline by:
   a use of **paragraphing**,
   b the **key words and ideas** (these should be underlined or noted),
   c **signpost words**, that is words which point out the direction of an argument, e.g. **though, how, although, on the other hand**.

3 Look closely at the words used. Check not only what they say but what they imply. Note particularly words which have a strong emotional flavour to them, e.g. **mob, skinny**, as distinct from **crowd** and **slim**.

4 Check the use of figurative language, that is language which contains similes and metaphors. Always ask why the simile or metaphor has been used and what is the effect of its use.

5 If there are words which you do not understand see if the context helps you, but do not jump to conclusions.

6 When answering questions in the practice exercises:
   a give the answers in sentences, unless otherwise asked,
   b if there is a suggested length of answer, keep to it,
   c avoid starting or answering with the words of the question as that often leads to difficulty,
   d if you are asked to quote then quote from the passage, otherwise use your own words as far as possible,
   e always check your answer with the question and the passage.

7 At the beginning of each of the following practice exercises an assessment level is indicated. This refers to the assessment guide on page 26, and is an indication to the level of response the questions call for. There are also marks indicated after each question and these need some explanation. They apply only when:
   a the work is done in the time indicated at the beginning of the questions,
   b there has been no discussion or help with the extract. If either or both of these are changed significantly then the marks may need to be altered.
   They are only raw scores and not percentages.

Check the marks available with your answer.

Close reading

You need to practise and learn how to recognise:
1 the main outlines of a passage,
2 how a passage develops,
3 the main ideas and supporting ideas,
4 the difference between a statement of fact and an opinion,
5 the writer's purpose and intentions,
6 what is actually achieved.

Adolf

When we were children our father often worked on the night-shift. Once it was spring-time, and he used to arrive home, black and tired, just as we were downstairs in our nightdresses. Then night met morning face to face, and the contact was not always happy. Perhaps it was painful to my father to see us
5 gaily entering upon the day into which he dragged himself soiled and weary. He didn't like going to bed in the spring morning sunshine.

But sometimes he was happy, because of his long walk through the dewy fields in the first daybreak. He loved the open morning, the crystal and the space, after a night down pit. He watched every bird, every stir in the trem-
10 bling grass, answered the whinnying of the peewits and tweeted to the wrens. If he could, he also would have whinnied and tweeted and whistled in a native language that was not human. He liked non-human things best.

One sunny morning we were all sitting at table when we heard his heavy slurring walk up the entry. We became uneasy. His was always a disturbing
15 presence, trammelling. He passed the window darkly, and we heard him go into the scullery and put down his tin bottle. But directly he came into the kitchen. We felt at once that he had something to communicate. No one spoke. We watched his black face for a second.

'Give me a drink,' he said.
20 My mother hastily poured out his tea. He went to pour it out into his saucer. But instead of drinking he suddenly put something on the table among the teacups. A tiny brown rabbit! A small rabbit, a mere morsel, sitting against the bread as still as if it were a made thing.

'A rabbit! A young one! Who gave it you, Father?'
25 But he laughed enigmatically, with a sliding motion of his yellow-grey eyes, and went to take off his coat. We pounced on the rabbit.

'Is it alive? Can you feel its heart beat?'

My father came back and sat down heavily in his armchair. He dragged his saucer to him, and blew his tea, pushing out his red lips under his black moustache.
30 'Where did you get it, Father?'

'I picked it up,' he said, wiping his naked forearm over his mouth and beard.

'Where?'

'It is a wild one!' came my mother's quick voice.

'Yes, it is.'
35 'Then why did you bring it?' cried my mother.

'Oh, we wanted it,' came our cry.

Read the first time quickly, the second time more slowly.

'Yes, I've no doubt you did –' retorted my mother. But she was drowned in our clamour of questions.

On the field path my father had found a dead mother rabbit and three dead
40 little ones – this one alive, but unmoving.

'But what had killed them, Daddy?'

'I couldn't say, my child. I s'd think she'd aten something.'

'Why did you bring it!' again my mother's voice of condemnation. 'You know what it will be.'

45 My father made no answer, but we were loud in protest.

'He must bring it. It's not big enough to live by itself. It would die,' we shouted.

'Yes, and it will die now. And then there'll be *another* outcry.'

My mother set her face against the tragedy of dead pets. Our hearts sank.
50 'It won't die, Father, will it? Why will it? It won't.'

'I s'd think not,' said my father.

'You know well enough it will. Haven't we had it all before!' said my mother.

'They dunna always pine,' replied my father testily.

55 But my mother reminded him of other little wild animals he had brought, which had sulked and refused to live, and brought storms of tears and trouble in our house of lunatics.

Trouble fell on us. The little rabbit sat on our lap, unmoving, its eye wide and dark. We brought it milk, warm milk, and held it to its nose. It sat as still
60 as if it was far away, retreated down some deep burrow, hidden, oblivious. We wetted its mouth and whiskers with drops of milk. It gave no sign, did not even shake off the wet white drops. Somebody began to shed a few secret tears.

'What did I say?' cried my mother. 'Take it and put it down in the field.'

Her command was in vain. We were driven to get dressed for school. There
65 sat the rabbit. It was like a tiny obscure cloud. Watching it, the emotions died out of our breast. Useless to love it, to yearn over it. Its little feelings were all ambushed. They must be circumvented. Love and affection were a trespass upon it. A little wild thing, it became more mute and asphyxiated still in its own arrest, when we approached with love. We must not love it. We must
70 circumvent it, for its own existence.

So I passed the order to my sister and my mother. The rabbit was not to be spoken to, nor even looked at. Wrapping it in a piece of flannel I put it in an obscure corner of the cold parlour, and put a saucer of milk before its nose. My mother was forbidden to enter the parlour while we were at school.

75 'As if I should take any notice of your nonsense,' she cried affronted. Yet I doubt if she ventured into the parlour.

Adolf D. H. Lawrence

Does the context help you with the meaning of a new word?

Practice

(Under 1 hour)
Level: questions 1 to 4 = levels 3 to 4; questions 5 to 7 = 1 to 3; questions 8
and 9 = 1 to 2

1 Describe the different contrasts in the first two paragraphs. (3)

2 What do lines 19–20 tell us about the relationship between husband
and wife? (2)

3 Describe the reaction of the rabbit when it was given the milk. (2)

4 What did the children then decide to do (lines 71–74)? (2)

5 Describe the attitude of the children towards:
a the father
b the mother
c animals (3 × 4)

6 Describe the father's character and what he looked like. (7)

7 Why do your think the miner had such feeling for the rabbit? (2)

8 Look at the way the mother speaks. How does it contrast with the
father's speech? (4)

9 Write a short paragraph on the way the author conveys feeling and
describes people. (6)

Total (40)

Check your answers with the questions and the passage.

Suggested marking scheme

For the passage *Adolf*, a suggested marking scheme is provided. Credit may be given for answers not indicated on a marking scheme, but which satisfactorily deal with the questions. After the marking scheme, one candidate's answers are given, plus comments. These should be used as a basis for discussion.

1 Contrasts:
night and morning
heavy work and joyfulness of nature
down the mine and open fields

2 He speaks to her in a rough manner.
She immediately does as he tells her.

3 It sat still as though it was in its burrow.
It took no notice when milk was put into its mouth.

4 As they had to get dressed for school they left it alone.
They realised it was numb with shock.
They decided not to smother it in love.
They wrapped it in flannel and put it in a corner.

5 Attitude to (**a**) father:
He was a disturbing presence for them.
They are in awe or fear of him.
They address him as father.
They are tense in his presence.
Once he stops being firm they are very open with him.
They take notice of what he says.
Attitude to (**b**) mother:
They are more relaxed with her.
They take no notice of her protests.
They take sides with the father over the rabbit.
They do not do as she tells them.
Attitude to (**c**) animals:
They like animals 'smothered them with love'.
They are considerate towards them.
They do not think of the consequences although they had obviously tried to keep wild animals in the past.

6 Physical:
black moustache and beard
yellow and grey eyes
impression of heavy walking
Character:
enjoys nature
sympathised with wild creatures
moody
enjoys surprising the family
speaks roughly to them
gets on better with animals than with human beings

Answer in sentences, unless told otherwise.

7 Finds it difficult to speak to people.
As a miner he knows what it is like to spend much time underground.

8 She is more precise in her language and does not shorten words, e.g. 'It is a wild one!'
He is abrupt and rough in the way he speaks and uses dialect forms.

9 By contrast, good description, choice of words, particularly unusual use of them.
'Passed the window darkly'.
The character's actions, 'blowing his tea'

Discussion of answers

The following are answers given by a candidate. Assess them and decide how many marks you would give each one. Following the answers are comments on them.

1 In the first paragraph it says that sometimes when he came back from working all night in the pit he was black and tired and would drag himself to bed and also that he did not like sleeping in on spring mornings. However in the second paragraph it says how he would come back from the pit whistling and talking to the animals.

Comment: This question will probably be answered best either by giving each set of contrasts in turn or by weighing one with the other. Such expressions as: **whereas, but, in contrast**, are useful. As there are only three marks, four to six lines should be sufficient.

2 The lines 19 and 20 tell us that the father was very much the master of the household and that his wife was quite scared of him.

Comment: The question refers to two lines of the passage and the answer should be based on them. Although the candidate's answer seems different from the marking scheme, is it satisfactory?

3 There was no reaction off the rabbit when it was given milk it didnt even shake off its whiskers

Comment: Only two marks again so the answers need to be accurate. Is 'no reaction' adequate?

4 The children decided to put the rabbit in a corner of the parlour with a saucer of milk at its nose and said that nobody was to look at it or touch it.

Comment: The line reference directs you to the part of the passage that contains the material of your answer. The marking scheme is a summary of the actions and credit can be given to actions not specifically stated, e.g. They told their mother not to touch it.

The difference between the metaphoric and literal use of words

5 a The children felt sorry for their father becaus he had to work in the pits at night and sleep during the day.

b The children probably did not like their mum as much as their dad because when their father brought them something home like the rabbit she would tell them that He should not have and that he should take it back.

c The children would get attached to the animals very quickly and would cry there eyes out if one died.

Comment: There is much material available to answer these questions but it needs interpreting. The candidate has not paid sufficient attention to the number of marks available. He should have realised that what he wrote for **5(a)** was inadequate.

6 The description of the father's character is that he had an unpredictable character one moment he would be happy and the next moment he would be sad or angry.
He has a black moustache and beard and yellow-grey eyes.

Comment: The physical description can be given in two to four lines but the character description calls for interpretation of the father's language and actions. The candidate has created difficulties for himself by starting his answer with the words of the question. Re-write the answer given.

7 I think the miner had such a feeling for the rabbit because they both spent a lot of their time in tunnels (pit) and they both slept during the day.

Comment: Although there are only two marks the answer needs to show interpretation and speculation based on the overall passage.

8 The mother speaks quickly and sharply and there father dosent use a lot of words to say what he wants to.

Comment: In order to answer this fully you need to quote in support of your statements.

9 The author describes the father as if he is very depressed with work at night and sleeping in the day. He describes the mother as not an evil woman but who is concerned about stopping the children being upset by the death of an animal, she unknowingly gets them to dislike him for not letting them have a pet.

Comment: If you are unsure of how much to write for such a question take the number of marks available as a general guide. This question asks for awareness of the writer's techniques. Description of the people is insufficient. This is a difficult task to do well.

Does the context change the meaning of a word?

General consideration

In giving marks for the answers, do the following influence you?

1 spelling mistakes
2 mistakes in grammar
3 awkwardly expressed answers
4 punctuation mistakes

Questions for quick reading passages (page 25)

Execution Dock

1 Where was Execution Dock?
2 Who were executed there?
3 What was the original manner of execution?
4 What was this changed to?
5 Why were bodies left there?
6 Who was the most famous person killed there?

Cost of trainers

1 Which trainers are the cheapest?
2 What are the main features of them?
3 What is the difference between the two Addidas brands?
4 Describe the dearest trainers.
5 What is the cost and description of the new brand?

Accident

1 At what time did it happen?
2 Name the roads.
3 What were the road conditions?
4 How did the accident happen?
5 Which driver was a woman?
6 Describe the injuries received.

Avoid starting your answer with the words of the question.

Running Scared

Passage A   The bus queue outside Goldings Comprehensive School was its usual push and
shove, pushing across the pavement to the railings and shoving with elbows
and plastic carriers towards the front. With one bus every twenty minutes, the
drivers preferring to stop short and turn round rather than make the school
5   pick-up, it was a frustrated scramble most afternoons. But horse-play, insults
and a bit of boy-girl business usually helped the time to pass.
       For two girls in the queue, though, for Paula Prescott and Narinder Kaur
Sidhu, the interval between buses seemed endless, the appeal of banter, nil.
Because Narinder's eyes hadn't seemed to leave the ground for days, and now
10   Paula's were starting to look somewhere else for friendship. Seven years
together might have been a long time, but it was as if the older racists had got
at them and suddenly the repartee, the quick laughs, the lightning looks which
said a lot, all these had almost gone. But since colour had never come between
them, what it was all about was hard to understand for Paula; while Narinder
15   didn't have any option but to keep quiet about something she didn't understand herself. So there was this depressing buffer in the middle of the queue,
two girls past whom the shouts and passings-on couldn't run, a deadening
effect like wet blankets at a party.
       The bus eventually arrived to a mix of cheers and abuse, and a surge forward
20   which threatened to throw someone under its wheels. From the top deck, two
pensioners on their way home from the bingo looked out at the queue and
pulled faces as the riot clattered up the stairs and rocked the bus on its springs.
Narinder and Paula slumped themselves into a seat in front of the old women
and noisy pairings went on all around, while Tommy Parsons and Scott Taylor
25   found themselves places as near to the two girls as they could, with only the
pensioners between them. Tommy stood up and leaned over, almost knocked
a wig out of place. 'You comin' out tonight then, Prescott?'
       Paula turned in her seat but put her face back to the front again before
answering. 'No, I ain't!'
30   'What about you, Nind? Meet me down the bench 'alf-seven?'
       Narinder flashed her eyes. She might have been miserable but when the top
deck suddenly went quiet she knew she had to reply. 'I wouldn't be seen *dead*
down the bench with you.'
       Tommy laughed and leaned over further. 'You don't need no dowry to come
35   out with me, you know!'
       'No, *I'd* need the paying! Get lost, Parsons!'
       Tommy jeered, but the sound was cut short by a look he got from one of
the women in front of him. 'Got your eye on the sixth-form, then, Nind?' he
tailed off: lame words which span Paula's head so fast to face Narinder that
40   something clicked in her neck.

Answer in your own words unless told otherwise.

'Here, is that what all the moody's about? You're not thinking of going out with no-one from the sixth-form, are you?'

'What, with my dad? I'm lucky to go out with my mum sometimes!' And Narinder snapped herself shut in her silence again, staring out of the window,
45 seeing nothing.

But Tommy couldn't let anything rest. 'Anyhow, Linda Bradley knows when she's well off!'

Paula laughed loud enough for downstairs to hear. 'What, with you? Well off her head, you mean!'

50 For reply Tommy and Scott whooped in derision and pushed to be first down the stairs, with a hand spare each for sign language at the girls. But it was quiet when they'd gone, and Paula tried for the millionth time to get some sort of sense from Narinder. 'Cheer up, Nind, it might never happen!' she started.

Narinder went on staring miserably out of the window. 'I think it already
55 has.'

'Why don't you come home to tea then? Watch my grandad finish that neck-lace he's making me.'

Narinder didn't even have the will to put much into her sigh. 'No, I can't,' she said, 'if it's not all fixed up before . . .'

60 'Yeah?' And Paula turned away to stare into the distance herself. She had tried, her long-suffering face seemed to say, but all she'd got was blanked. And what use were friends if they couldn't tell each other things? She looked round at Narinder again, at the sad, dead expression on her face. And her eyes soft-ened, her head tipped sympathetically to one side. What was it that was
65 changing Nindy from the brilliant mate she'd been into this zombie who'd just as soon stare at nothing as look her best friend in the face?

Can you distinguish between fact and opinion?

Passage B

In one of the shopping streets between Paula's house and the corner where the raid was planned to take place, Narinder's father had set up his small printing business. It had been a greengrocer's when he'd bought it, but there were greengrocers everywhere, it had seemed, while there were very few
5 people prepared to supply the printing needs of a rapidly growing Asian community . . . which was handy, as Narinder would have said, seeing that Pratap Singh Sidhu had trained as a young man at the London School of Printing. So he had set himself up. But like plenty of others in difficult times, he was feeling the pinch these days – and not only the pinch of the govern-
10 ment's economic policies: there were other things going on as well which were both emptying the till and draining Pratap of some of the courage he'd once been famous for.

Protection, that was the name of the game. The protection racket. The smiling, matey face which threatened a razor if you didn't smile back. Soft
15 words wrapped round hard threats, like muffling round a gun. So the big greengrocery windows were painted black to above eye level, and customers had to ring and be recognised these days before Pratap would let them in. None of which, of course, was any good for business; and wasn't much better for family life, not when it meant that no-one could go out except in the bright-
20 ness of day, and they all had to give a coded ring to get themselves let back in.

And this was what was depressing Narinder: seeing her dad going downhill, feeling all this edginess at home, and not understanding any of the reasons why except what she could see for herself – that he was running scared of
25 something.

Tonight she had Paula with her, had persuaded her on the bus after the boys had gone to leave her necklace for half an hour and come and have some tea with her. It was the least she could do, seeing how moody she'd been all day. Besides, she always liked taking Paula into her bedroom, never got tired of
30 her saying how it was special, got a lift every time from knowing it had a style her friend had never found anywhere else. Because she *was* different, and this room showed just where she stood in the world, with its framed picture of Guru Nanak all bright on one side and Bruce Springsteen on the other: with a long-necked sitar propped up against the stereo. And it was her own room,
35 too – Paula always went on about that. Being an only child wasn't always a drawback.

The tea grouts were cold now, and Paula would have to be going, but another family's photo-album is always intriguing, and Narinder's was more than most, especially coming out now: because these Sikh wedding pictures,
40 outdoor in India, showed Nindy's parents as such beautiful, carefree people, like film stars, and very different to the unhappy couple downstairs.

'Here, look at your mum. Weren't she pretty?' Paula's eyes said it all, how it always gives your stomach a turn to see a beautiful bride, that weird feeling at the mix of religion and sex. 'Looks happy, don't she?'
45 'She does there. It's different now.'

Paula looked up sharply as if that was it, the reason for the long faces suddenly made clear: as if Narinder was trying to bring it out in the open in

---

Read over what you have written and correct errors.

these pictures. Was there something up with Nindy's dad and mum in a man and wife sort of way? Was that the problem?

50 'No, nothing like that!' Nindy's brown eyes widened, she wrinkled her fine nose. 'Something else.' She waved her arms wide.

'The business?' Paula started to nod, looked relieved that it wasn't family. 'My dad and my grandad have bad weeks, cabbing. They wouldn't give a smile to a baby sometimes, neither of 'em.'

55 But Narinder hadn't really stopped shaking her head from the question before. 'No, it's . . . Paula, it's big: it's ever so big, I know it is!' She dropped her voice, looked at her friend with a new serious look on her face. And as she looked Narinder knew she hadn't been stupid to bring Paula here: because it seemed so much more real, the feel of the danger here in the house, and 60 it was helping her to speak about it – helping her to take the chance to keep hold of her old friend. 'I tell you for nothing, Paula, my dad's real scared about something round her, something . . . *heavy* . . . you know! And it's killing us, Paula, our family . . .' And then she could say no more, just because there was no more which she knew to say; and because now, for the first time in 65 front of anyone else, she was crying.

'All right, Nind, all right, mate.' Paula was comforting, cuddling her. 'Head up, girl – we'll lick it. You've got me – remember?'

And just for that Narinder knew she'd been right to share her mysterious fear.

Running Scared Bernard Ashely

Practice

(Under 1 hour)
Level: mainly 3 and 4, but questions 6, 11 and 13 = 1 to 4

Passage A

1 Describe in your own words the general behaviour of the pupils as they waited for the bus. (2)

2 Why do you think some bus drivers tried to avoid picking up pupils? (2)

3 How long had Paula and Narinder been friends and what were the signs that the friendship was breaking up? (3)

4 Describe the attitude of Tommy Parsons towards the girls. (3)

5 What does the reference to Linda Bradley (lines 46–47) hint at? (2)

6 What impressions do you get from this passage of Tommy's character? (4)

Passage B

7 Describe how the protection racket worked. (2)

Should a question mark be inside or outside speech marks?

8 Give three reasons why Pratap had changed the type of shop he had. (3)

9 Which part of Passage B explains Narinder's remark in Passage A that she could not go out? (2)

10 What was special about Narinder's room? (3)

11 Why was she depressed and how is the reason for it gradually revealed? (6)

12 Between the two extracts another group of characters are introduced. What were they discussing? (2)

13 How does the way the two girls talk to each other show that they are close friends? Give examples. (6)

Total (48)

One candidate's answers

Read the following answers to the questions on *Running Scared*. Assess how many marks you would give each answer and which level (1 to 4) you would award them overall.

1 They very noisy, messing about and shouting.

2 There buses were full.

3 They had been friends for a very long time but now they didn't seem to be talking to each other.

4 He didn't think much of them.

5 That she'd been out with him and fancied him.

6 He's a big head who thinks he is god's gift to girls.

7 If the owner of the shop didn't pay the money they would send round some guys who'd wreck it or razor them.

8 They already had enough greengrocers.
They needed a printers.
He was scared of the protection racket.

9 My dad's real scared of something round here, something heavy you know.

10 It had a lot of pop posters but also a lot of Indian stuff.

11 She was afraid that her dad was in danger.
It is gradually revealed by letting you know it bit by bit.

12 A robbery.

13 They talk like as if they were friends. Paula calls Narrinder Nind and mate and Narrinder lets her into her secret.

Read the passage at least twice.

The Great Mouse Plot

Passage A   My four friends and I had come across a loose floor-board at the back of the class-
room, and when we prised it up with the blade of a pocket-knife, we discovered
a big hollow space underneath. This, we decided, would be our secret hiding
place for sweets and small treasures such as conkers and monkey-nuts and
5   birds' eggs. Every afternoon, when the last lesson was over, the five of us would
wait until the classroom had emptied, then we would lift up the floor-board and
examine our secret hoard, perhaps adding to it or taking something away.

   One day, when we lifted it up, we found a dead mouse lying among our
treasures. It was an exciting discovery. Thwaites took it out by its tail and
10   waved it in front of our faces. 'What shall we do with it?' he cried.

   'It stinks!' someone shouted. 'Throw it out of the window quick!'

   'Hold on a tick,' I said. 'Don't throw it away.'

   Thwaites hesitated. They all looked at me.

   When writing about oneself, one must strive to be truthful. Truth is more
15   important than modesty. I must tell you, therefore, that it was I and I alone
who had the idea for the great and daring Mouse Plot. We all have our
moments of brilliance and glory, and this was mine.

   'Why don't we,' I said, 'slip it into one of Mrs Pratchett's jars of sweets?
Then when she puts her dirty hand in to grab a handful, she'll grab a stinky
20   dead mouse instead.'

   The other four stared at me in wonder. Then, as the sheer genius of the plot
began to sink in, they all started grinning. They slapped me on the back. They
cheered me and danced around the classroom. 'We'll do it today!' they cried.
'We'll do it on the way home! *You* had the idea,' they said to me, 'so *you* can
25   be the one to put the mouse in the jar.'

   Thwaites handed me the mouse. I put it into my trouser pocket. Then the
five of us left the school, crossed the village green and headed for the sweet-
shop. We were tremendously jazzed up. We felt like a gang of desperados
setting out to rob a train or blow up the sheriff's office.

30   'Make sure you put it into a jar which is used often,' somebody said.

   'I'm putting it in Gobstoppers,' I said. 'The Gobstopper jar is never behind
the counter.'

   'I've got a penny,' Thwaites said, 'so I'll ask for one Sherbet Sucker and one
Bootlace. And while she turns away to get them, you slip the mouse in quickly
35   with the Gobstoppers.'

   Thus everything was arranged. We were strutting a little as we entered the
shop. We were the victors now and Mrs Pratchett was the victim. She stood
behind the counter, and her small malignant pig-eyes watched us suspiciously
as we came forward.

40   'One Sherbet Sucker, please,' Thwaites said to her, holding out his penny.

Incorrect speling should luck odd.

I kept to the rear of the group, and when I saw Mrs Pratchett turn her head away for a couple of seconds to fish a Sherbet Sucker out of the box, I lifted the heavy glass lid of the Gobstopper jar and dropped the mouse in. Then I replaced the lid as silently as possible. My heart was thumping like mad and
45 my hands had gone all sweaty.

'And one Bootlace, please,' I heard Thwaites saying. When I turned round, I saw Mrs Pratchett holding out the Bootlace in her filthy fingers.

'I don't want all the lot of you troopin' in 'ere if only one of you is buyin',' she screamed at us. 'Now beat it! Go on, get out!'

50 As soon as we were outside, we broke into a run. 'Did you do it?' they shouted at me.

'Of course I did!' I said.

'Well done you!' they cried. 'What a super show!'

I felt like a hero. I *was* a hero. It was marvellous to be so popular.

Passage B   The flush of triumph over the dead mouse was carried forward to the next morning as we all met again to walk to school.

'Let's go in and see if it's still in the jar,' somebody said as we approached the sweet-shop.

5 'Don't,' Thwaites said firmly. 'It's too dangerous. Walk past as though nothing has happened.'

As we came level with the shop we saw a cardboard notice hanging on the door.

We stopped and stared. We had never known the sweet-shop to be closed at
10 this time in the morning, even on Sundays.

'What's happened?' we asked each other. 'What's going on?'

We pressed our faces against the window and looked inside. Mrs Pratchett was nowhere to be seen.

'Look!' I cried. 'The Gobstopper jar's gone! It's not on the shelf! There's
15 a gap where it used to be!'

'It's on the floor!' someone said. 'It's smashed to bits and there's Gobstoppers everywhere!'

'There's the mouse!' someone else shouted.

We could see it all, the huge glass jar smashed to smithereens with the dead
20 mouse lying in the wreckage and hundreds of many-coloured Gobstoppers littering the floor.

'She got such a shock when she grabbed hold of the mouse that she dropped everything,' somebody was saying.

'But why didn't she sweep it all up and open the shop?' I asked.

25 Nobody answered me.

We turned away and walked towards the school. All of a sudden we had begun to feel slightly uncomfortable. There was something not quite right

Capital letters for people's names

about the shop being closed. Even Thwaites was unable to offer a reasonable explanation. We became silent. There was a faint scent of danger in the air
30 now. Each one of us had caught a whiff of it. Alarm bells were beginning to ring faintly in our ears.

After a while, Thwaites broke the silence. 'She must have got one heck of a shock,' he said. He paused. We all looked at him, wondering what wisdom the great medical authority was going to come out with next.
35 'After all,' he went on, 'to catch hold of a dead mouse when you're expecting to catch hold of a Gobstopper must be a pretty frightening experience. Don't you agree?'

Nobody answered him.

'Well now,' Thwaites went on, 'when an old person like Mrs Pratchett sud-
40 denly gets a very big shock, I suppose you know what happens next?'

'What?' we said. 'What happens?'

'You ask my father,' Thwaites said. 'He'll tell you.'

'You tell us,' we said.

'It gives her a heart attack,' Thwaites announced. 'Her heart stops beating
45 and she's dead in five seconds.'

For a moment or two my own heart stopped beating. Thwaites pointed a finger at me and said darkly, 'I'm afraid you've killed her.'

'*Me*?' I cried. 'Why just *me*?'

'It was *your* idea,' he said. 'And what's more, *you* put the mouse in.'
50 All of a sudden, I was a murderer.

The Boy Roald Dahl

Practice

(Under 1 hour)
Level: mainly 3 and 4, but questions 5 and 9/10 = 1 to 4

Passage A

1 What does the word 'treasures' tell us about the boys' attitude to the objects they hid? (2)

2 This passage could give you the impression that the writer was big-headed as a boy.
a Identify the statements which seem to support this.
b Do you think that he was big-headed? (4)

3 Why are capital letters used for Mouse Plot? (1)

4 How do you know that the author did not like Mrs Pratchett? (2)

5 Write four to five lines describing your impression of her. (3)

Check the marks available with your answer.

Passage B

6 Point out the stages by which the author's feelings change from triumph in the first line to the feelings in the last line. (4)

Both

7 How old do you think the boys were and on what do you base your answer? (2)

8 Using evidence from both passages what sort of boy was Thwaites? (3)

Writing

Choose one of the following:

9 Mrs Pratchett's Revenge. Write your own account how this could have taken place. (9)

or

10 Give a full account of a practical joke you were involved in which went wrong. (9)

Total (30)

One candidate's answers

What level would you award the following?

1 It shows you how much they value them.

2 a The sheer genius of the plot
   We all have moments of brilliance and this was mine.
   b I think he was more showing off than big headed.

3 Because it's important.

4 From the way he discribes her. He says she had pig eyes and filthy fingers.

5 I think she was horrible with her little piggy eyes. She was like a lot of shopkeepers who think all kids go in just to nick things. She had dirty hands and picked the sweets up with them. She shouted a lot.

6 First he thinks he's the big hero but when they see the shop closed they start wondering. When they see the dead mouse they stop talking, then they become a little scared. Thwaites keeps on saying what would happen to an old woman who'd had a great shock. He says she would have a heart attack and the writer had murdered her.

7 I think they were very young about 9 or 10 because of the way they talk and the silly trick they play.

8 Thwaites is the sort of boy you get everywhere. He always wants to be the boss and leader (Passage A, lines 33–35). He also likes to impress the others with his superior knowledge but he rubs it in a bit and exaggerates to make the author uncomfortable.

The difference between 'quote' and 'in your own words'

The Poltergeist

Beautiful golden Joanna had been with the Beckets for two months when the noises began. At first there were loud bangs and cracks, at night. Soon they were heard in the daytime too, and then the first object was hurled by an invisible hand across the room – a favourite plate of Mrs Becket's that shat-
5 tered against a green glass vase, which broke too.

They were all in the room at the time, and from that moment on there was no use pretending any more. They had a poltergeist.

The strangeness had been creeping up on them for a long time. Jane could not remember exactly when she had first begun to feel a faint uneasiness, but
10 it had certainly been after Joanna's arrival.

The circumstances of her coming to stay with the Beckets had in themselves been odd. The family had already taken in one evacuee, briefly. Billy was eight, and came to them because his parents had been killed in the bombing and at the time his relatives could not be traced. Then an aunt had been
15 located in Scotland, and he had gone to her.

'But keep my name on the list,' Mrs Becket had told Miss Frobisher, who was organising the placing of children in that district. 'It would be lovely if we could have a girl – somewhere about Jane's age. Such company, her being an only.'

20 Certainly for as long as she could remember Jane had longed for a sister, someone to play, plan and gossip with. She had visualised this sister only in the vaguest outline, but whatever she had expected it had certainly been nothing like Joanna.

When her mother first told her of the new arrival, Jane was enchanted.

25 'As a matter of fact, she may be a little difficult,' Mrs Becket said. 'I don't quite know what the trouble is, but apparently this will be her third move in only a couple of months.'

'What – you mean she's a real tearaway?' Jane liked the sound of this, though she could see that her mother might not.

30 'I'm not exactly . . . well, Miss Frobisher was really rather vague. She assured me that the girl wasn't any trouble in herself. It was simply that she couldn't seem to fit in with the other families. Poor child. It's really very sad. Fancy being moved from pillar to post like that! Anyway, we'll have to try specially hard to make her feel at home here. And you most of all.'

35 'Of course!' Jane said. 'There's no need to *tell* me! I bet we'll get on like a house on fire.'

(Later, that remark was to seem remarkably like a prophecy.)

Jane spent the next few days trying to make the spare room attractive. In other words, making it look as she herself would like it. She took pictures,
40 books and old cuddly toys from her own room and arranged them carefully on the walls and shelves. And on the day Joanna was to arrive she picked flowers from the garden for the dressing table. She took one last look round before leaving for the station with her mother.

'Perfect!' she decided. 'Looks as much like home as *mine* does!'

The Poltergeist Helen Cresswell

Capital letters for names of countries, towns, cities

Practice

(Under 1 hour)
Level: mainly 4 and 3; question 7 = 1 to 4

1 From the account given in lines 1–7 what do you think a poltergeist is? (2)

2 The word 'evacuee' (line 12) is not explained, but there are plenty of clues in the passage. What are they and what does it mean? (3)

3 Why did Jane want a girl evacuee? (2)

4 Why did Mrs Beckett feel sorry for Joanna? (2)

5 What evidence is there that Jane is a kind-hearted girl? (3)

6 Consider how the story line develops.
   a What do the first three words suggest about Joanna? (1)

   b Where is it implied that the poltergeist was connected with Joanna? (1)

   c What does the statement in brackets (line 37) suggest? (2)

7 Now using all your answers to the above suggest how the story goes on and finishes. In the original story there is a happy ending. (9)

Total (25)

Read the first time quickly, the second time more slowly.

Fudge

The next day it rained. My father asked me how I'd like to go to the movies.

'Just me?' I asked.

'No. All three of us,' he said.

'Fudge is very young to go,' I said. 'Don't you think so?'

5 'Maybe. But I can't think of anything else to do with him. And that will take up a few hours.'

'You could give him some socks,' I suggested. 'You know how he loves to play with your socks.'

'Socks won't last the whole afternoon,' my father said. 'That's why I thought
10 of the movies.'

'What'll we see, Dad?'

My father checked his *New York* magazine. '*A Bear's Life* is playing in the neighbourhood. How does that sound?'

'What's it about?' I asked.

15 'A bear's life, I guess,' my father said. 'It's rated G.'

I was thinking of a good Western with lots of action or else a picture rated R where you can't get in if you're under seventeen unless you're with your parents. But my father had made up his mind. *A Bear's Life* it was.

I suggested that my father get Fudge cleaned up. Because by then he was
20 looking kind of messy. I don't think my father even put him into his pyjamas last night. He's been wearing the same polo shirt ever since my mother left yesterday morning.

By one o'clock we were ready to go. All three of us wore our raincoats and boots and my father took his big, black umbrella. One thing about New York
25 – it's hard to get a cab when it's raining. But the movie theatre wasn't very far away. My father said the walk would do us all good. There were a lot of puddles. It was really pouring. I like to walk in the rain. Especially if it isn't too cold out. It feels nice when it wets your face.

I jumped over the puddles. My father avoided them too. But not Fudge. He
30 jumped right into every one and splashed around like a little duck. By the time we got to the movie theatre the bottoms of his pants were soaked. My father took him into the men's room. He stuffed a bunch of paper towels up each pant leg so Fudge wouldn't have to sit around wet. At first Fudge complained. But when my father bought him a big box of popcorn he forgot about his stuffed pants.

35 Right after we got settled in our seats a big boy sat down in front of Fudge so he had to change seats with my father. Now he was on the aisle, I was in the middle, and my father was on my other side.

When the lights dimmed Fudge said, 'Ohhh . . . dark.'

I told him, 'Be quiet. You can't talk in the movies.'

40 'Okay, Pee-tah,' he said.

That's when he started throwing his popcorn. At first I didn't notice but wondered why the people in front of us were turning around every second. Then I heard Fudge whisper, 'Pow-pow-pow!' and I saw him throw a handful of popcorn.

45 I poked my father. 'He's throwing his popcorn,' I whispered.

My father reached across me and tapped Fudge on the leg. 'If you throw one more piece I'm going to take it away from you.'

Its' is always wrong.

'No throw!' Fudge said very loud.

'Shush. . . .' the people in front of us said.

50   'Shush!' Fudge said back to them.

'You see,' I told my father, 'he's too young for the movies. He doesn't understand.'

But from the moment the first bear came on the screen Fudge sat still and watched. And after a while I forgot all about him and concentrated on the
55   movie. It was much better than I thought it would be. It showed all these bear cubs and how they live.

I'm not sure when I realized Fudge was gone. I guess it was when I turned to ask him if he had any popcorn left. I had already finished mine and was still hungry. I was really surprised to see he wasn't there. I mean, one minute he
60   was sitting right next to me and the next minute he was gone.

'Hey, Dad,' I whispered to my father. 'He's gone.'

'What?' my father said.

Should this have a question mark

'Fudge isn't in his seat.'

My father looked over. 'Where did he go?'

65 'I don't know. I just noticed he was gone.'

'Let me out, Peter. I'll find him.'

'Should I come too?' I asked.

'No . . . you can sit here and watch the rest of the picture. He's probably wandering around by the candy counter.'

70 I stood up to let my father out. I wondered what my mother would think if she knew Fudge was lost in the movies.

A few minutes later the picture stopped – right in the middle of a scene. The sound track trailed off like a broken record. All the lights came on. The audience let out a groan. Some kids called, 'Boo . . . boo!'

75 Then my father and two ushers and a man in a suit came over to me. 'He was sitting right here,' my father told them, pointing to the empty seat on the aisle.

'Well,' the man in the suit said, 'we've checked the rest rooms and the office. He's not behind the candy counter. We'll have to search the theatre.' He

80 cupped his hands around his mouth and shouted, 'Ladies and gentlemen . . . may I have your attention please. We'll continue with our film in one moment. But first we have to find a three-year-old boy answering to the name of Fudge.'

Some people laughed when the man said his name. I guess *Fudge* does sound funny if you're not used to it. I thought, *Maybe he's been kidnapped! Would*

85 *my mother be mad. That crazy kid! You can't even take him to the movies.* Then I thought, *Who'd want to kidnap him, anyway?*

'What should I do, Dad?' I said.

'Why don't you walk up and down this aisle and call him, Peter.'

'Okay,' I said.

90 'Here, Fudge,' I called, starting down my aisle. I sounded like I was calling a dog. 'Come on out, Fudge.'

When I got down to the first row and called, 'Here, Fudge,' he popped out at me. He scared me so bad I yelled, 'Ooooh. . . .'

'Hi, Pee-tah,' he said.

95 'Hey . . . I found him,' I called. 'I found him . . . I found him . . . here he is!' Then I turned to my brother. 'You dope! What are you doing way down here? And why are you sitting on the floor?'

'Wanted to touch the bears,' Fudge said. 'But bears are all gone.' He spread out his arms and said, 'All gone' again.'

100 My father and the ushers and the man in the suit ran to us. 'Fudge,' my father said, scooping him up. 'Are you all right?'

'He wanted to pet the bears,' I said. 'Can you beat that?'

'Well, I guess we can continue with the picture now,' the man in the suit said. He cupped his hands around his mouth again. 'Thank you, ladies and

105 gentlemen. Our young man has been found safe and sound. Now we return to the conclusion of *A Bear's Life.*'

My father carried Fudge back to our seats. He held him on his lap for the rest of the show. I guess he wasn't taking any more chances!

Tales of a Fourth Grade Nothing Judy Blume

Don't use a comma where you should have a full stop,

Practice

(Under 1 hour)
Level: questions 1 to 6 = 3 to 4; question 8 = 1; questions 9 and 10 = 1 to 4

1 Why did they go to the movies? (1)

2 What does this tell us about the father's attitude to Fudge? (2)

3 Explain the difference between the G and R ratings for films. (2)

4 How did it come about that Fudge sat in the seat near the aisle? Why was this careless? (4)

5 Describe what Fudge did when he got away. (3)

6 Apart from the reference to New York, what other indications are there that the writer is American? (2)

7 Would you say that Fudge was a badly behaved child who easily got his own way? (2)

8 How does the author make this embarrassing incident amusing? (8)

9 Imagine you are Peter and you have to tell your mother what happened. Use dialogue and include in your account what your feelings were. (8)

10 Describe a similar experience, either of yourself when young or of a member of your family. (8)

Total   (40)

Answer in sentences, unless told otherwise.

FUDGE

1. Peter, Fudge and their father all went to the movies because it was something to keep Fudge occupied for a few hours.

2. This tells that their father does not quite know how to cope with a young child and that he is not used to looking after Fudge. He takes Fudge to the movies to keep him quiet and because he has not got anything better to do with Fudge and so he (the father) can have, a bit of piece and quiet.

3. G rated films are films anyone can see, no matter what age you are or who accompanies you. R rated films are films you can only see if you are 17 or over unless an adult accompanies you.

4. To begin with, Fudge was sitting in the seat next but one to the aisle, his father in the seat next to the aisle. Then a big boy came and sat in front of Fudge so now Fudge could not see the screen. Then Fudge and his father swapped seats and now Fudge was next to the aisle. This was careless because Fudge could have swapped seats with Peter or could have sat on his fathers knee. His father should have realised that Fudge could run away sitting next to the aisle.

5. Fudge got away very quietly as Peter did not realised that Fudge had escaped straight away. After he had got away he went down the aisle to the first row and hid. He went

there so that he could pet the bears. Fudge stayed hidden there while the film stopped until he jumped out on Peter whom was walking down the aisle looking for him.

6. Other indications that the author is american are the references to 'movies' where in England you say 'cinema' or 'pictures'. The ratings - G and R - are different to the ones used in England. The author refers to 'cab' as opposed to 'taxi' and 'mens room' as opposed to 'Gentlemens toilet'

7. Yes, Fudge is a badly behaved boy who easily gets his own way. His father tries to control him by bribes like going to the movies or popcorn. Fudge is spoilt and shows off like when he shouted "no throw" in the cinema.

8. The author makes the embarrassing incident amusing by some of the things that Peter thinks or says "Maybe he's kidnapped" "Would my mother be mad". As if a mother would not be mad that the little boy was missing "Who'd want to kidnap him anyway?" This makes out that Fudge is just a nuisance not worth bothering with. It is also amusing by things Fudge did like jumping into all the puddles or wanting to pet the bears. Some of the things Fudge says and his mannerisms add some humour, as does the way the author brings out that Fudge is a spoilt kid who is at his father's wits end. The way Peter hunts for Fudge is funny as it is like someone looking for a lost dog, as are some of the similes and

Where is place; were the plural of was

comparisons the author uses like Fudge 'splashing around like a little duck in the puddles.'

9. "Dad decided to take us to the movies. Not a good idea. Fudge is too little, but we still went. Anything for a peaceful life I suppose.
"It was raining outside and Fudge had to jump into the puddles. He was soaked by the time we got to the movie theatre. After Dad had tried to dry him we went and sat down. Fudge ended up sitting in the seat next to the aisle so he could see. Another mistake.
"Anyway the film began and Fudge started to throw the popcorn that Dad had bought him. Dad stopped him eventually, but I thought to myself that Fudge is too young for the movies.
"Then Fudge got bored and decided to go for a little walk. After a bit I noticed that he had disappeared. I started to get worried. Dad went to look for him and the film had to be stopped so the theatre could be searched. You can imagine what happened then. Lots of people started booing and were angry.
"I wondered what you would be thinking if you had known what was happening. I started walking up and down the aisles shouting for Fudge. I felt really stupid. Everyone was staring at me. It was like I was looking for a lost dog. When I got to the front row Fudge jumped out on me. The little brat scared the life out of me. Fudge's explaination was that he'd only gone there to pet the bears in the movie.
"Dad took charge of Fudge and we returned to our seats. Fudge was placed on Dad's knee.

Why hadn't he been there all the time?!"

While I had been telling mum the story she said nothing. But now she laughed and remarked "I see I won't be leaving Fudge and your Dad alone for a while!"

12. One bright Sunday morning Peter, who was then two, decided to come to church with us. So armed with sweets, biscuits, toys and anything to keep Peter quiet mum and I left for church. Dad was left at home, he could not stand the stress. "We are going to see Father Keane and Father Brogan," I had told Peter previously. So once in the church Peter started shouting at the top of his voice "See Brogan and Keane, Brogan and Keane." It sounded like a firm of soliciters. "Sshh," mum told Peter. Peter put his hand to his mouth and said, "Sssh. Be quiet Peter."

10 minutes of the service passed with Peter sitting quietly on the bench sandwiched in between mum and myself. Then he got bored I think, and he started shouting "There's Father Keane. Hallo." Talk about embarrassing. I could see people looking around for where this outburst had come from. However the offertory hymn saved us from any more of Peter's outburst but Peter, being Peter did something else. He innocently stood on the bench and started dancing and swaying on the bench to the music. The people in the row behind us were giggling. Peter was turning this solemn service into a circus act. Then the hymn ended. "More music" wailed Peter. Then

Incorrect speling should luck odd.

dummy shoved in mouth, fruit pastilles in hand, he shut up.

Peace was restored until the altar boy rung the bell and Peter perked up with, "Phone, Ring! Ring! Phone nanna." The church had been deadly silent and Peter's little voice resounded around it. Why did we bring Peter with us?

The next embarrassing incident happened a few minutes later. An old woman was kneeling down praying, her face in her hands. Peter swivelled around on the bench and peered through the lady's hands. "'Allo" he said, in an inquisitive, appealing voice. "'Allo lady." I clenched my teeth and pulled Peter away trying to surpress my giggles and remain obscure.

Wasn't I pleased when everything was over I don't think Peter would be coming to church for a bit.

Language to suit your purpose and audience

Counterfeit

The spaceship plunged through the black starways towards the orbit of the third planet. Its trip had been long. It was homeward bound.

Donald Shaver sat staring at the navigation board, his face grey. He gazed at the space-charts, and a tremor shook his narrow shoulders.

5 A tall, blond man swung open the hatch and sauntered into the navigation shack, beaming. 'Ho, Donnie!' he bellowed. 'We're off that blasted sink-hole at last, eh? What do you think of that?' He glanced by habit at the bright red dot on the navigation board, then turned and peered happily out of the observation port, rubbing his hands in anticipation.

10 'I wish I were home,' said Shaver, dully.

The blond man laughed. 'You and eighty others! Don't worry, laddies, we're on the way. Just another week now, and –'

The boy's voice cut in with urgency. 'I wish I were home *now*.' He took another breath, and unmistakable shudder shook his body. The blond man

15 turned, his eyes widening in alarm.

'Donnie!' he said softly. 'What's wrong, laddie?'

'I'm sick, Scotty!' he whispered. 'Oh, Scotty, please, get the Doc – I'm awful sick!' He shook in another uncontrollable tremor, losing his grip on the table and toppling forward.

20 The tall Scot caught him as he fell, easing him down to the deck. 'Hold on, Donnie,' he whispered. 'I'll take care o' you.' The boy doubled up suddenly in a paroxysm of coughing, choking, his face blue. His back arched and twisted in convulsion; then, abruptly, he relaxed.

Scotty crossed the room, snatched up a phone from the table, rang it franti-

25 cally. 'Navigation to Central,' he snapped. 'Get the Doc up here in a hurry. I think –' He glanced, wide-eyed, at the still form on the deck. 'I think a man just died!'

Dr John Crawford leaned back in the relaxer, spreading his long legs out in front of him, and stared glumly out of his observation port. He had been

30 sitting there for over an hour, his slender fingers toying with the greyish cards in his hands, staring, and smoking, and scowling. For the first time in the long voyage he felt tired, and alone, and afraid.

The doctor might have been handsome, had he shaved, and changed into

---

The difference between the metaphoric and literal use of words

35 a fresh Exploratory Command uniform. He was a lanky man, his gaunt face hardened by the dark stubble of two day's beard, while a shock of jet black hair, uncombed, contributed to the air of preoccupied concern that hung about him. 'Dr Ponderous', one of the men had called him, in an unguarded moment, and he had chuckled to himself as he walked away.

40 That was probably the picture the men on the ship had of him – slow of speech, possibly a little dull, a reasonably pleasant and harmless fellow who seemed too big to be walking around the corridors of a spaceship. Dr Crawford knew it wasn't true, of course. He was just careful. A ship's doctor on an exploratory mission had to be careful, in every thought and action. The great, disease-gutted hulks of a dozen earlier exploratory ships had proved that, very
45 conclusively.

Dr Crawford started from the port, watching the unblinking white pinpoints of starlight on the black-velvet background, his frown deepening. To have called the trip unsuccessful, from any viewpoint, would have been mild. After all the anticipation, all the excitement, it had been a dud. A complete, miser-
50 able, hopeless dud, from beginning to end. No glory. No discovery. Nothing.

Until an hour ago.

He stared at the cards in his hands. Just an hour ago Jenson, the Chief Hospitalman, had brought the cards to him, panting from the run up from the laboratory, and Dr Crawford had taken them, and studied them, and felt fear
55 gnawing at his stomach.

Suddenly he jumped from the relaxer, and started down the darkened corridor toward the skipper's cabin. He saw the light over the hatch, indicating that the skipper was in, and his hand shook as he rang the bell. An impossible thing to take to the skipper – and yet, he knew he had no choice.
60 Captain Robert Jaffe looked up as the doctor entered the cabin, and his round, dark face broke into a grin. The doctor bent to avoid banging his head in the hatchway, and walked across to the skipper's desk. Try as he would, he couldn't muster a smile, and he saw Captain Jaffe's eyes grow serious as he sank into a relaxer. 'What is it, Doc?'
65 'We've got trouble, Bob.'

'Trouble? After this trip?' He grinned and leaned back. 'Don't be silly. What kind of trouble?'

'We've got an extraordinary man aboard, Bob.'

The captain shrugged, raising his eyebrows. 'We have eighty extraordinary
70 men aboard. That's why they came on this trip –'

'I don't mean *that* kind of extraordinary. I mean downright unbelievable, Bob. We've got a man on this ship, walking around, robust and healthy, who *ought to be dead.*'

'That's an odd thing for a doctor to say,' he said cautiously. 'What do you
75 mean?'

Crawford waved the grey cards at him. 'It's right here,' he said. 'These are lab reports. As you know, I ordered a complete physical examination on every man aboard, the day after we blasted from Venus. A normal procedure – we had to be sure that nothing had been picked up by the exploring parties, or
80 anybody else. Among other things, we ran complete lab studies on each of the

Lose the opposite of find, but loose is not tight.

men – urine, blood chemistry, and so forth. We got every man on board into the lab within two days after blasting, and took blood samples from them. And we got some remarkable results.'

Jaffe drew on his cigarette, watching the doctor impatiently.

85 'There are eighty-one men on the ship,' the doctor continued. 'Of these, eighty presented a clean bill of health, absolutely negative reports on everything. But one man was slightly different.' He tapped the cards with a slender finger. 'One man showed everything normal – blood count, chlorides, calcium, albumin-globulin ration – everything just the way it should be. Then we ran 90 his blood sugar.' The doctor stretched his leg, regarding his toes closely. 'This man didn't have any blood sugar,' he said. 'Not a trace.'

Captain Jaffe stiffened, his eyes suddenly wide. 'Now wait a minute – I'm no doctor, but even *I* know –'

'– that a man can't live without any blood sugar.' The doctor nodded his head. 95 'You're so right. But that wasn't all. After we couldn't find any blood sugar, we ran a test for blood creatinin. That's a protein-breakdown product, rapidly disposed of, and if it ever gets as high as 10 milligrams per hundred cc's of blood, the patient is in trouble. I've *never* seen a creatinin higher than twenty-five, and that man was dead when the blood was drawn. A man with a crea-100 tinin level that high *has* to be dead, he *couldn't* be alive –' He paused for a moment, wiping a trickle of sweat from his forehead. 'This man's test ran 135 –'

Counterfeit Alan E Nourse.

Practice

(More than 1 hour)
Level: questions 1 to 3 = 3 to 4; question 6 = 1 to 4; questions 4, 5, 7 and 8 = 1 to 2

1 What is the first indication that something is wrong? (1)

2 What contrast is established between Donald and Scotty? (3)

3 What is the nature of their mission and how exciting had it been? (2)

4 Give a brief description of the doctor's character. Why was he a good choice for a space mission? (5)

5 How does his temperament add weight to what he tells the captain? (2)

6 Describe in your own words the situation which was worrying the doctor. (4)

7 How effective is this extract as an opening of story? Refer in your answer to the situation, events, characters and moods. (10)

8 From the information given and remembering the title give an outline of how you think the story could develop and end. (6)

Total (33)

Would you prefer to be long and lanky or tall and slim?

At the End of April

The sun still waits in the back of the sky,
But it's warmer now; great bunches of leaves
Come shouldering, clambering
Up through the earth, overnight it seems –
5 To be ready for poppies, perhaps,
Or stiff stalks of golden plate.

The birds, now perfectly certain,
Speed low over the Green, with beaks clamped tight
On difficult bits for nests;
10 While beneath their flight
The wicket is being carefully cut and measured
For an early game.

Old people emerge from winter to sit
Again round the edge of the Green;
15 And when they lean forward to talk,
Or throw bread to the birds, or sniff the twirling
Cuttings of grass, they lean away
From the lettering carved on the backs of their seats –

Words that say
20 Given in Memory of one who loved to sit
Here on the Green, and watch cricket –
Or the spring coming; or their time
Going; or whatever it was they
Saw in the afternoons.

Susanah Amoore

Does the context change the meaning of a word?

Practice

(Under 1 hour)
Level: full range 1 to 4 for all questions

1 What does the first line imply? (2)

2 What are the signs of spring and of warmer days? (6)

3 Why are the birds 'now perfectly certain' (line 7)? (2)

4 What is the connection between the bench with the writing on it and the old people? (2)

5 What contrasts are stated or implied between spring and old age? (4)

6 Consider the following statements about the poem and say whether you agree with them or not and give reasons for your opinions.
   a The poet has a good eye for detail.
   b There is little point in the poem – only a description of old people watching the first cricket match of the season.
   c The poet is really saying that memorials are a waste of time and money, for life has to go on.
   d The poem criticises old people for just sitting around doing nothing. (12)

Total (28)

Have you covered the topic as fully as possible in the time?

Miss Smith

One day Miss Smith asked James what a baby horse was called, and James couldn't remember. He blinked and shook his head. He knew, he explained, but he just couldn't remember. Miss Smith said:

'Well, well; James Machen doesn't know what a baby horse is called.'

5 She said it loudly so that everyone in the class-room heard. James became very confused. He blinked and said:

'Pony, Miss Smith?'

'Pony! James Machen says a baby horse is a pony! Hands up everyone who knows what a baby horse is.'

10 All the right arms in the room, except James's and Miss Smith's, shot upwards. Miss Smith smiled at James.

'Everyone knows,' she said. 'Everyone knows what a baby horse is called except James.'

James thought: I'll run away. I'll join the tinkers and live in a tent.

15 'What's a baby horse called?' Miss Smith asked the class, and the class shouted:

'Foal, Miss Smith.'

'A foal, James.' Miss Smith repeated. 'A baby horse is a foal, James dear.'

'I knew, Miss Smith. I knew but . . .'

20 Miss Smith laughed and the class laughed, and afterwards nobody would play with James because he was so silly to think that a baby horse was a pony.

James was an optimist about Miss Smith. He thought it might be different when the class went on the summer picnic or sat tightly together at the Christmas party, eating cake and biscuits and having their mugs filled from big

25 enamel jugs. But it never was different. James got left behind when everyone was racing across the fields at the picnic, and Miss Smith had to wait impatiently, telling the class that James would have to have his legs stretched. And at the party she heaped his plate with seed cake, because she imagined so she said, that he was the kind of child who enjoyed such fare.

30 Once James found himself alone with Miss Smith in the class-room. She was sitting at her desk correcting some homework. James was staring in front of him, admiring a fountain pen that the day before his mother had bought for him. It was a small fountain pen, coloured purple and black and white. James believed it to be elegant.

35 It was very quiet in the class-room. Soundlessly, Miss Smith's red pencil ticked and crossed and underlined. Without looking up, she said: 'Why don't you go out and play?'

'Yes, Miss Smith,' said James. He walked to the door, clipping his pen into his pocket. As he turned the handle he heard Miss Smith utter a sound of

40 irritation. He turned and saw that the point of her pencil had broken. 'Miss Smith, you may borrow my pen. You can fill it with red ink. It's quite a good pen.'

James crossed the room and held out his pen. Miss Smith unscrewed the cap and prodded at the paper with the nib. 'What a funny pen, James!' she said.

45 'Look, it can't write.'

'There's no ink in it,' James explained. 'You've got to fill it with red ink, Miss Smith.'

Don't use a comma where you should have a full stop,

But Miss Smith smiled and handed the pen back. 'What a silly boy you are to waste your money on such a poor pen!'

50 'But I didn't . . .'

'Come along now, James, aren't you going to lend me your pencil sharpener?'

'I haven't got a pencil sharpener, Miss Smith.'

'No pencil sharpener? Oh James, James, you haven't got anything, have
55 you?'

When Miss Smith married, James imagined he had escaped her for ever. But the town they lived in was a small one and they often met in the street or in a shop. And Miss Smith, who at first found marriage rather boring, visited the
60 school quite regularly. 'How's James?' she would say, smiling alarmingly at him. 'How's my droopy old James?'

Then, when Miss Smith had been married for about a year she gave birth to a son, which occupied her a bit. He was a fine child, eight pounds six ounces, with a good long head and blue eyes. Miss Smith was delighted with
65 him, and her husband, a solicitor, complimented her sweetly and bought cigars and drinks for all his friends. In time, mother and son were seen daily taking the air: Miss Smith on her trim little legs and the baby in his frilly pram. James, meeting the two, said: 'Miss Smith, may I see the baby?' But Miss Smith laughed and said that she was not Miss Smith any more. She wheeled the pram
70 rapidly away, as though the child within it might be affected by the proximity of the other.

'What a dreadful little boy that James Machen is!' Miss Smith reported to her husband. 'I feel so sorry for the parents.'

'Do I know him? What does the child look like?'

75 'Small, dear, like a weasel wearing glasses. He quite gives me the creeps.'

Almost without knowing it, James developed a compulsion about Miss Smith. At first it was quite a simple compulsion: just that James had to talk to God about Miss Smith every night before he went to sleep, and try to find out from God what it was about him that Miss Smith so despised. Every night
80 he lay in bed and had his conversation, and if once he forgot it James knew that the next time he met Miss Smith she would probably say something that might make him drop down dead.

After about a month of conversation with God James discovered that he had found the solution. It was so simple that he marvelled he had never thought
85 of it before. He began to get up very early in the morning and pick bunches of flowers. He would carry them down the street to Miss Smith's house and place them on a window-sill. He was careful not to be seen, by Miss Smith or by anyone else: he knew that if anyone saw him the plan couldn't work. When he had picked all the flowers in his own garden he started to pick them from
90 other people's garden. He became rather clever at moving silently through the gardens, picking flowers for Miss Smith.

Unfortunately, though, on the day that James carried his thirty-first bunch of blooms to the house of Miss Smith he was observed. He saw the curtains move as he reached up to lay the flowers on the window-sill. A moment later

Are you behind with your assignments?

95　Miss Smith, in her dressing-gown, had caught him by the shoulder and pulled him into the house.

'James Machen! It would be James Machen, wouldn't it? Flowers from the creature, if you please! What are you up to, you dozey James?'

James said nothing. He looked at Miss Smith's dressing-gown and thought
100　it was particularly pretty: blue and woolly, with an edging of silk.

'You've been trying to get us into trouble,' cried Miss Smith. 'You've been stealing flowers all over the town and putting them at our house. You're an underhand child, James.'

James stared at her, and then ran away.

105　After that, James thought of Miss Smith almost all the time. He thought of her face when she caught him with the flowers, and how she had afterwards told his father and nearly everyone else in the town. He thought of how his father had had to say he was sorry to Miss Smith, and how his mother and father had quarrelled about the affair. He counted up all the things Miss Smith
110　had ever said to him, and all the things she had ever done to him, like giving him seed cake at the Christmas party. He hadn't meant to harm Miss Smith as she said he had. Giving people flowers wasn't unkind; it was to show them you liked them and wanted them to like you.

'When somebody hurts you,' James said to the man who came to cut the
115　grass, 'what do you do about it?'

'Well,' said the man, 'I suppose you hurt them back.'

'Supposing you can't, James argued.

'Oh, but you always can. It's easy to hurt people.'

'It's not, really,' James said.

120　'Look,' said the man, 'all I've got to do is to reach out and give you a clip on the ear. That'd hurt you.'

'But I couldn't do that to you. Because you're too big. How d'you hurt someone who's bigger than you?'

125　'It's easier to hurt people who are weaker. People who are weaker are always the ones who get hurt.'

'Can't you hurt someone who is stronger?'

The grass-cutter thought for a time. 'You have to be cunning to do that. You've got to find the weak spot. Everyone has a weak spot.'

130　'Have you got a weak spot?'

'I suppose so.'

'Could I hurt you on your weak spot?'

'You don't want to hurt me, James.'

'No, but just could I?'

135　'Yes, I suppose you could.'

'Well then?'

'My little daughter's smaller than you. If you hurt her, you see, you'd be hurting me. It'd be the same, you see.'

'I see,' said James.

Miss Smith William Tevor

Formal English for formal occasions.

Practice

(More than 1 hour)
Level: full range 1 to 4 for all questions

1 Give an account of the different ways Miss Smith was unkind to James.　(6)

2 Describe what his feelings towards her were like at first and show how they changed.　(6)

3 Look at the incident of the fountain pen (lines 30–55).
　a What aspects of her character does it show?　(2)

　b Why was James particularly hurt by it?　(2)

4 What brings about the change in his attitude to her?　(2)

5 Summarise the conversation with the man cutting the grass. What do you think is the point of it?　(6)

6 Judging from the extract how do you think the story develops and ends?　(6)
　　　　　　　　　　　　　　　　　　　　　　　　　　Total　(30)

Avoid starting your answer with the words of the question.

The Wolf said to Francis

Francis was a famous preacher who had a great love for wild animals and this poem refers to one of the many legends about him when he tried to teach the wolf to be less savage and to love people.

The wolf said to Francis
'You have more sense than some.
I will not spoil the legend;
Call me, and I shall come.

5   But in the matter of taming
Should you not look more near?
Those howlings come from humans.
Their hatred is their fear.

We are an orderly people.
10 Though great our pain and need,
We do not kill for torture;
We do not hoard for greed.

But the victim has the vision –
A gift of sorts that's given
15 As some might say, by history
And you, perhaps, by heaven.
Tomorrow or soon after
(Count centuries for days)
I see (and you may also
20 If you will turn your gaze) –

How the sons of man have taken
A hundredfold their share.
But the child of God, the creature,
Can rest his head nowhere.

25 See, sky and ocean empty,
The earth scorched to the bone;
By poison, gun, starvation
The last free creature gone.
But the swollen tide of humans
30 Sweeps on and one and on.

No tree, no bird, no grassland
Only increasing man,
And the prisoned beasts he feeds on –
Was *this* the heavenly plan?'

Words have meaning and associations.

35 Francis stood there silent.
Francis bowed his head.
Clearly passed before him
All that the wolf had said.

Francis looked at his brother
40 He looked at the forest floor.
The vision pierced his thinking,
And with it, something more
That humans are stony listeners.

The legend stands as before.

A. G. Rochelle

Practice

(Under 1 hour)
Level: Full range 1 to 4 for all questions

1 What does the wolf say Francis would be better doing? (2

2 What accusation does the wolf level at human beings? (4

3 Describe the future as the wolf sees it. (4

4 What contrast is being made by the two phrases 'sons of man' (line 21) and 'child of God' (line 23)? (2

5 What is the point of the last line? (2

6 What is the attitude of many people towards wolves and how has this attitude been formed? What use does the poet make of it in the poem? (4

7 Explain what is meant or suggested by the following?
  a 'Their hatred is their fear' (line 8)
  b 'Count centuries for days' (line 18)
  c 'Humans are stony listeners' (line 43) (6

8 Do you agree with what the poet says in this poem? (6
Total (30

The difference between 'quote' and 'in your own words'

By St Thomas Water

By St Thomas Water
Where the river is thin
We look for a jam-jar
To catch the quick fish in.
5 Through St Thomas Church-yard
Jessie and I ran
The day we took the jam-pot
Off the dead man.

On the scuffed tombstone
10 The grey flowers fell,
Cracked was the water,
Silent the shell.
The snake for an emblem
Swirled on the slab,
15 Across the beach of sky the sun
Crawled like a crab.

'If we walk,' said Jessie,
'Seven times round,
We shall hear a dead man
20 Speaking underground.'
Round the stone we danced, we sang,
Watched the sun drop,
Laid our hearts and listened
At the tomb-top.

25 Soft as the thunder
At the storm's start
I heard a voice as clear as blood,
Strong as the heart.
But what words were spoken
30 I can never say,
I shut my fingers round my head,
Drove them away.

'What are those letters, Jessie,
Cut so sharp and trim
35 All round this holy stone
With earth up to the brim?'
Jessie traced the letters
Black as coffin-lead.
'*He is not dead but sleeping*,'
40 Slowly she said.

'Read the first time quickly. The second time more slowly.'

I looked at Jessie,
Jessie looked at me,
And our eyes in wonder
Grew wide as the sea.
45 Past the green and bending stones
We fled hand in hand,
Silent through the tongues of grass
To the river strand.

By the creaking cypress
50 We moved as soft as smoke
For fear all the people
Underneath awoke.
Over all the sleepers
We darted light as snow
55 In case they opened up their eyes,
Called us from below.

Many a day has faltered
Into many a year
Since the dead awoke and spoke
60 And we would not hear.
Waiting in the cold grass
Under a crinkled bough,
Quiet stone, cautious stone,
What do you tell me now?

Charles Causley

Does the context change the meaning of a word?

Practice

(Under 1 hour)
Level: questions 1–3 = 3 to 4; the rest = 1 to 4

1 Why did the two children go into the churchyard? (1)

2 What do lines 7 and 8 seem to say and what do they really mean? (2)

3 What is line 11 describing? (1)

4 Look at lines 17–32.
  a What does Jessie suggest they should do? (1)

  b How does the poet indicate that they did not take it seriously. (2)

  c What in effect happened and how did the boy react? (3)

5 How did they interpret the writing on the gravestone (line 39)? (2)

6 If, for line 57, the poet had written 'Many years have now gone by' what
suggestions would have been lost? (2)

7 Say what the last four lines mean to you. (4)

8 Say what you think the poet suggests by using the following words (you
need to give more than the meanings).
'scuffed' (line 9) 'grey' (line 10)
'I heard a voice as clear as blood' (line 27) 'tongues of grass' (line 47) (6)

9 Choose two similes or metaphors (but not those in question 8) and
explain what you think the poet is trying to achieve by them and how
successful he is. (6)

                                              Total (30)

Answer in your own words unless told otherwise.

Albert and the Probation Officer

In the following extract Mr Stokes is a probation officer. He has to investigate the background of a boy called Albert Braxton who is in trouble. He has written to Albert's father in Brixton, but has not received a very welcoming reply i.e. 'Come if you want to. E. Braxton.'

The roads between Peckham Rye and Dulwich are of interminable length, and, as always in my case, the address I sought seemed to be purposely elusive. But eventually I found myself outside the door of the neat suburban villa I was looking for, and banged on it with what energy I had left. Nothing happened.
5 I banged again, with the same result; and then, gingerly stepping on to a flower-bed, I peered in through the window. As there was nobody inside the room it was absurd of me to knock on the pane, but knock I did, as if half expecting the inmates suddenly to crawl out from under a sofa or come up through a trap-door. And because I refused to believe that I might have made
10 the journey for nothing, I knocked again, more loudly. It was then that a piping voice behind me asked if I was a burglar trying to break into the house. The voice belonged to a boy of about six, who regarded me with obvious suspicion.

'Does Mr Braxton live here?', I asked with a smile, which was not returned.
15 'You've trodden on my daisy plants', said the boy, in whose small face I now recognized an unmistakable likeness to Albert's. 'Aren't you clumsy!'

Lifting my feet from the crushed flowers, I apologized, and repeated the question.

'Dad's out the back', said the boy and disappeared.
20 The side entrance of the house led to a strip of back-garden in the centre of which a large man was tinkering with an upturned bicycle. I remember that he had a nearly bald head, and the flattened nose of a bruiser. I remember many other things about him that I wish I could forget, for nobody likes to be reminded of the humiliations he had suffered.
25 'Are you Mr Braxton?', I asked, with what I'm afraid was something very akin to a Sunbeam's jollity.

'Could be', was the curt reply.

'I'm Mr Stokes. I've come to see you about Albert.'

'Have you now?'
30 I felt I wasn't going to like Albert's dad, whose identity needed no further proof. *Le style est l'homme même.* And here, unmistakably, was the author of 'Come if you want to. E. Braxton.' I was deciding whether to challenge his impertinence, or ignore it altogether, when Albert's dad said, without turning his head:
35 'Second puncture I've had this week . . . Kids put tin-tacks on the road . . . If I catch one of them I'll tan the hide off him.'

But I wasn't going to be side-tracked.

'About Albert', I said doggedly.

'What about him?'
40 'I like Albert.'

'Glad someone does.'

Does the context help you with the meaning of a new word?

'I understand him.'

'First one who has.'

'He's coming out in two weeks.'

45 'More's the pity.'

'And he wants to come home.'

'He can want.'

Apart from the locale, we might have been conversing in a comedy by Noel Coward. The bicycle claimed its owner's sole attention. I saw that if I were

50 to get any of it, a provocative note must be introduced.

'After all,' I said, 'was Albert's crime as bad as it was made out to be? Assault on police. Any of us might have done the same thing; in a spirit of fun, of course.'

'Would you?', asked Albert's dad.

55 'Actually, I wouldn't.'

'No more would I.'

'But I'm inclined to think, Mr Braxton, that the police were just as much to blame as your son. From what Albert tells me, they know him around here and watch out for him. When they see him go into a pub they wait until he

60 comes out. I'm afraid it's a case of *agent provocateur* you know.'

'Agent my arse', said Albert's dad indignantly; but his attention remained on the bicycle.

Had I known it, then was the moment to give the whole thing up as a bad job, to call it a day so far as Peckham was concerned. The trousers Albert's

65 dad was wearing ought to have warned me that I was playing with fire. But I was not experienced in such matters then. One pair of dark blue legs looked very like another.

'I've nothing against the police, if you understand me?'

'I'm trying to.'

70 'But I suppose it is a part of their job to get knocked about a bit.'

'And part of Albert's to do the knocking?'

'I don't mean that exactly.'

'Then what the hell do you mean?'

The man's interest was aroused at last. And turning on me a face puce with

75 anger, he said, in the deliberate tone of one who does not intend to be misunderstood:

'Are you aware, Mr Stokes, that when he was brought into the charge-room by the four officers it had taken to arrest him, Albert broke away from them and attacked the station-sergeant? And do you know that when those officers

80 had lifted Albert off the station-sergent, the station-sergeant had both eyes closed up, his front teeth knocked in – and his nose broken?'

'I didn't know', I said, after quite a long pause.

'I thought not. And there's just one other thing I'd like to tell you: I was the station-sergeant.'

85 Confusion covered me in a big way. With downcast eyes I notice, too late, those tell-tale uniform trousers above the sergeant's boots; and I decided to impress upon Albert that in future he must learn to be more explicit in his talk. When I lifted my head it was to find the small boy back again. He clasped a

---

Lead (leed); lead metal

90 bucket filled with water. I can't think why I remember that Donald Duck's hideous face was on it. I smiled mechanically at the boy. He smiled back at me. And then, taking great care not to avoid his target, he emptied the bucket's entire contents over my shoes.

'That's for treading on my daisy plants', he said, and disappeared.

95 Squelching my way homewards, I tried to believe in a divine justice that might reveal Albert's brother as the kid who had put the tin-tacks on the road, and that Albert's dad would tan the hide off him for his trouble.

Court Circular Sewell Stokes

Practice

(More than 1 hour)
Level: full range 1 to 4, but questions 8 and 9 more demanding.

1 What qualities of the author do we see in the first paragraph? How would they help him to do his job? (3)

2 What was the author's first impression of Mr Braxton? (2)

3 Show how Mr Braxton's attitude to Mr Stokes is conveyed in the first part of their conversation (lines 25–50). (5)

4 Why does the author try to excuse Albert's behaviour? (2)

5 How did this make matters worse? (2)

6 What clue about Mr Braxton's identity did he ignore? (1)

7 Which statements would have been particularly annoying to Albert's father? (3)

8 What does the small boy add to this incident? (4)

9 How does the author achieve a gradual build up to his final discomfort?(Look at the dialogue, the three characters involved, the tension between them and the clues ignored.) (8)

10 *Either* describe how you would feel in a similar situation and how you would try to get out of it; *or* give an account of a situation in which you made a fool of yourself. (8)

Total (38)

Check your answers with the questions and the passage.

The Titanic

Read the extract and the poem.

TITANIC, **R.M.S.**, a White Star liner of 46,328 tons, was the largest ship in the world when she was built. She struck an iceberg in the North Atlantic on her maiden voyage in 1912 and sank with the loss of 1,490 lives. Built to safety
5   flotation standards higher than required by regulations then or now, and with sixteen water-tight compartments, she was regarded as virtually unsinkable. She sailed on her maiden voyage from Southampton to New York on 10 April 1912. On the 14th, nearing the Grand Banks, she received four warnings from ships of ice ahead, but the last one, describing a field right across her track,
10   never reached the captain. As usual in clear weather she steamed on at her

service speed of 22 knots throughout the evening. There are rumours, but no evidence, that she was out to break records; in fact she had insufficient coal aboard to try. At 11.40 p.m. the crow's nest lookout reported an iceberg close ahead and the First Officer immediately ordered a full turn to port. The bows
15 missed the iceberg, but an underwater spur of ice ripped an intermittent gash down her starboard side extending 300 feet and puncturing six forward compartments. She could not survive this damage, but the passengers were not told for fear of panic. Board of Trade regulations for lifeboats had not kept pace with the increased size of ships, and while there were 2,201 persons
20 aboard, the lifeboats could only hold 1,178. The boats were, however, lowered only partly filled with passengers who refused at first to believe the ship would or could sink.

SOS wireless signals were sent, and rockets were fired when a light appeared on the horizon at about 1.00 a.m. on the 15th. But the light moved away and
25 the nearest ship to receive the SOS, the Cunard liner *Carpathia*, could not reach the scene before 4.00 a.m. The *Titanic*, after settling slowly by the bows, sank at 2.20 a.m. leaving 916 passengers and 673 crew to die in the icy water. The passengers who lost their lives included 106 women and 52 children, nearly all from the third, or emigrant, class; the crew lost included all the engineer
30 officers who were working below until the last moments. The *Carpathia* rescued 712 persons from the *Titanic's* boats.

Unprecedented shock and horror greeted the news, and two inquiries into the disaster found a scapegoat in the captain of the steamer *Californian*, which they stated was the source of the light seen on the horizon at 1.00 a.m. The
35 evidence is quite clear that the light could not have come from this ship. Captain Smith of the *Titanic* was not blamed as it was not normal practice for liners to reduce speed in clear weather. There is no reason to question this finding; it is likely that the iceberg had recently overturned and was showing a dark side; there was no wind or swell to create ripples around it. It was an
40 accident, and blame is a product of hindsight and ignorance of the customs of the day. More important, the disaster led to new regulations requiring ships to carry sufficient lifeboats for all carried on board, a more southerly liner track across the Atlantic, and an ice patrol which continues to this day.

The Oxford Companion to Ships and the Sea

The tattered remnant of a glittering chandelier within the sunken Titanic. ▶

Formal English for formal occasions.

The Convergence of the Twain

(Lines on the loss of the *Titanic*)

I

In a solitude of the sea
Deep from human vanity,
And the Pride of Life that planned her, stilly couches she.

II

Steel chambers, late the pyres*
Of her salamandrine* fires,
Cold currents thrid,* and turn to rhythmic tidal lyres.

III

Over the mirrors meant
To glass the opulent
The sea-worm crawls – grotesque, slimed, dumb, indifferent.

IV

Jewels in joy designed
To ravish the sensuous mind
Lie lightless, all their sparkles bleared and black and blind.

V

Dim moon-eyed fishes near
Gaze at the gilded gear
And query: 'What does this vaingloriousness down here?' . . .

* See question 10

VI

Well: while was fashioning
This creature of cleaving wing,
The Immanent Will that stirs and urges everything

VII

Prepared a sinister mate
For her – so gaily great –
A Shape of Ice, for the time far and dissociate.

VIII

And as the smart ship grew
In stature, grace, and hue,
In shadowy silent distance grew the Iceberg too.

IX

Alien they seemed to be:
No mortal eye could see
The intimate welding of their later history,

X

Or sign that they were bent
By paths coincident
On being anon twin halves of one august event,

XI

Till the Spinner of the Years
Said 'Now!' And each one hears,
And consummation comes, and jars two hemispheres.

Thomas Hardy

Does the context help you with the meaning of a new word?

Practice

(More than 1 hour)
Level: questions 1 to 9 = 4 and 3; questions 10 to 15 = mainly 1 to 4

Titanic, R.M.S. (i.e. Royal Mail Ship)

1 Why was the *Titanic* regarded as unsinkable? (1)

2 Look at lines 18–22.
   a Why was there a shortage of lifeboats?
   b Why were some not filled? (2)

3 Why was the danger of this situation not fully realised? (1)

4 Write out a time log of the events, e.g.
   10th April, 1912
   14th April
        11.40 p.m. .... (4)

5 Describe the damage caused by the iceberg. What loss of life was there? (3)

6 Why were the losses greater than they need have been? (2)

7 Explain what the writer of the article means by
   a 'scapegoat' (line 33)
   b 'blame is a product of hindsight' (line 40) (2)

The Convergence of the Twain

8 What does the title refer to? (1)

9 Find two expressions similar in meaning in the poem. (2)

10 Stanza II (lines 4 to 6) seems difficult at first.
   A pyre is a pile of wood on which a dead body is burnt.
   Salamandrine refers to a type of lizard which was supposed to be able to survive in a fire.
   Thrid is on old-fasioned form of threaded.
   Using the above information, what is the author trying to suggest in the lines? (4)

11 What examples of human vanity are given? (3)

12 What is the effect of introducing the sea worms and fishes into the picture? (4)

13 How is the suddenness of the crush emphasised? (4)

14 Pick any group of three lines in which the repetition of the rhyme drives home the meaning and explain how it does. (4)

Both passages

15 The first passage is factual and the second is an imaginative reconstruction of the facts. How effective is each one in its own way and which do you find more effective overall? (8)
                       Total (45)

Can you distinguish between fact and opinion?

Showbiz Charts

Passage A

Showbiz has always thrived on the romantic notion of the over-night rags-to-riches sensation. It is a well-worn cliché to which publicists, entertainment journalists and the writers of B movie scripts frequently resort. Yet, in reality, success is rarely quite as instant as they would all have us believe. Except in

5 the world of pop. There it *is* a common phenomenon. In fact, it is probably fair to say that it is the rule rather than the exception.

One week a group can be flogging up and down the motorways in a beat-up van playing in dingy clubs and halls for a pittance that hardly covers the cost of their petrol or transport cafe breakfast; the next week they are stars

10 who can command up to £500-a-night.

What makes the difference is a hit record. A No 1 hit guarantees a small fortune and opens up the possibility of a vast one. The minimum £100,000 that can be expected from British sales is only the tip of the iceberg. Lucrative licensing deals can immediately be negotiated for the release of the record in

15 those other countries throughout the world where it also has a good chance of becoming a hit.

And, of course, nothing succeeds like success. Once a group has made that initial breakthrough they automatically gain the impetus necessary to set up a snowball effect. When their next record comes out it is virtually assured of

20 the attention and airplay essential to the creation of a hit but which – as unknowns – they would have found much more difficult to attract. It is true that there are a few so-called one-hit wonders. But it is equally true that there are *no* no-hit wonders.

When so much depends on getting into the charts it is hardly surprising in

25 a notoriously cut-throat business that there are those who are not prepared to leave it to chance. For the unscrupulous, fixing the charts has never presented that much of a problem.

Would you prefer to be long and lanky or tall and slim?

Passage B

It is a reasonably reliable system although obviously a long, long way from being 100 per cent accurate. But then neither *NME** nor *Melody Maker* has ever claimed to be more than just a guide. For a long time nobody argued too violently with this. The charts were, after all, just a bit of fun intended to cater
5 innocently for that same fascination for statistics that gives the sporting league tables their immense appeal. By the mid-Sixties, however, the charts were no longer being taken quite so lightly – certainly not by those within or close to the record business. There were two main reasons for this. One was the enormous expansion of the pop industry during the Beatle era. The other, even
10 more important, was the broadcasting revolution that ushered in the age of non-stop radio pop. This was started by the pirate stations and then the BBC capitulated with the introduction in 1967 of 'onederful' Radio 1.

These two developments combined to focus much greater public interest on the charts and also to increase vastly their influence over the music business
15 as a whole. Not only was a much more widespread audience of children, housewives, factory workers and motorists being bombarded with a constant barrage of chart statistics but the BBC were basing their programming on these statistics. At the same time the dealers began to rely on them more and more as a guide to what discs they should order from the deluge of output released
20 each week.

The charts were not just for fun any more. Too much depended on them.

* New Musical Express.

Passage C

Although nominally a Top Fifty, the BMRB* chart is in effect a Top Sixty. The last ten placings are occupied by the so-called 'star breakers' which are the ten next best-selling *new* records – as against ones which are on the way down the chart.
5 Beside each title is recorded its total sales in the panel shops that week. Because the Top Five records alone account for more than 30 per cent of all singles sales in an average week – No 1 = 9.9 per cent, No 2 = 7.5 per cent, No 3 = 5.5 per cent, No 4 = 4.5 per cent and No 5 = 4 per cent – the margin between each of these top records tends to be quite considerable.
10 But, the further down the chart you get, the tinier the margins between each position become. Nos 30–50 and the star breakers share between them a very small percentage of the total sales. So they are often divided by only a handful of sales.

* British Market Research Bureau

Sharon told Gillian she was wrong. Who was wrong?

For example, a fairly typical chart showed No 1 with sales of 3,442, No
15 with 3,128, No 3 with 2,606, No 4 with 2,061 and No 5 with 1,814. But, at the
other end, No 40 sold only 345, No 41 = 340, No 42 = 331, No 43 = 323
No 44 = 314, No 45 = 303, No 46 = 293, No 47 = 263, No 48 = 243, No 4
= 237 and No 50 = 234.

In other words, as the size of the sample at this time was 300 shops
20 Nos 46–50 sold an average of less than one copy in each of the chart shops.

In theory, therefore, by buying just two or three copies of a record at aroun
half of the chart shops one could boost it into the low forties without the ai
of a single legitimate sale. The pattern of sales would be sufficiently uniforr
to avoid arousing suspicion. And, to make fairly certain of satisfying th
25 BMRB's random double-check, one would merely have to go 'shopping' at
sensible selection of the non-panel stores. If a record is anyway selling reasor
ably well – although not quite well enough to guarantee chart entry – then th
hype becomes even more simple.

People might joke about their mum being the only person to buy thei
30 record. But it would be quite feasible to nudge a record from nowhere int
the all-important star breakers – or from the star breakers into the Top Fift
– just by getting a few members of one's family to go out and buy one cop
each.

In the particular chart already referred to the fifth star breaker sold 20
35 copies while the No 50 notched 234. Even a small family of 30 would hav
served to put that breaker in at No 49. A decent collection of cousins and
could have been pushed considerably higher.

The Pop Industry Inside Out M. Cable

Be clear – be precise – be accurate.

Practice

(More than 1 hour)
Level: questions 1 to 3 = 3 and 4; the rest = 1 to 4

Passage A

1 Explain clearly in your own words what the following mean.
   a 'well-worn cliché' (line 2)
   b 'tip of the iceberg' (line 13)
   c 'initial breakthrough' (line 18)
   d 'snowball effect' (line 19)   (4)

2 What major argument is put forward in paragraph one?   (2)

3 There are many colloquial expressions in the passage, i.e. expressions
   only used in conversation but not in formal English.
   a Identify four such expressions.   (2)

   b Why do you think the writer uses such language?   (1)

4 Describe what happens when a record is No 1 in the charts.   (3)

Passage B

5 Why were the charts originally compiled?   (2)

6 What two developments changed this?   (4)

7 Explain how too much eventually depended on the charts.   (2)

Passage C

8 Which sentence in Passage A is Passage C an amplification of?   (1)

9 Panel shops are the selected record shops which supply a weekly return with
   a number of discs sold. Summarise the way the BMRB chart is compiled. (3)

10 Explain what 'starbreakers' are?   (2)

11 Explain how it is easy to fix the charts.   (4)

12 The following statements refer to the information in the
   passages. Say whether each statement is true, false or partially true,
   and give the reasons on which you base your answer:
   a It is common to find showbusiness people becoming very wealthy
      overnight.   (2)

   b A No 1 hit record guarantees a vast fortune.   (2)

   c Some very successful pop groups have not had any hit records. (2)

   d The system for compiling the record charts is not absolutely reliable. (2)

   e The record shops have the main reason for fixing the charts. (2)
                                                          Total   (40)

Capital letters for names of countries, towns, cities

On the Train

Dora got into the train. It was now very full indeed and people were sitting four a side. Before she sat down she inspected herself quickly in the mirror. In spite of all her awful experiences she looked good. She had a round well-formed face and a large mouth that liked to smile. Her eyes were a dark slaty blue
5 and rather long and large. Art had darkened but not thinned her vigorous triangular eyebrows. Her hair was golden brown and grew in long flat strips down the side of her head, like ferns growing down a rock. This was attractive. Her figure was by no means what it had been.

She turned towards her seat. A large elderly lady shifted a little to make
10 room. Feeling fat and hot in the smart featureless coat and skirt which she had not worn since the spring, Dora squeezed herself in. She hated the sensation of another human being wedged against her side. Her skirt was very tight. Her high-heeled shoes were tight too. She could feel her own perspiration and was beginning to smell that of others. It was a devilish hot day. She reflected all
15 the same that she was lucky to have a seat, and with a certain satisfaction watched the corridor fill up with people who had no seats.

Another elderly lady, struggling through the crush, reached the door of Dora's carriage and addressed her neighbour. 'Ah, there you are, dear, I thought you were nearer the front.' They looked at each other rather gloomily,
20 the standing lady leaning at an angle through the doorway, her feet trapped in a heap of luggage. They began a conversation about how they had never seen the train so full.

Dora stopped listening because a dreadful thought had struck her. She ought to give up her seat. She rejected the thought, but it came back. There was no
25 doubt about it. The elderly lady who was standing looked very frail indeed and it was only proper that Dora, who was young and healthy, should give her seat to the lady who could then sit next to her friend. Dora felt the blood rushing to her face. She sat still and considered the matter. There was no point in being hasty. It was possible of course that while clearly admitting that she
30 ought to give up her seat she might nevertheless simply not do so out of pure selfishness. This would in some ways be a better situation than what would have been the case if it had simply not occurred to her at all that she ought to give up her seat. On the other side of the seated lady a man was sitting. He was reading his newspaper and did not seem to be thinking about his duty.
35 Perhaps if Dora waited it would occur to the man to give his seat to the other lady? Unlikely. Dora examined the other inhabitants of the carriage. None of them looked in the least uneasy. Their faces, if not already buried in books, reflected the selfish glee which had probably been on her own a moment since as she watched the crowd in the corridor. There was another aspect to the
40 matter. She had taken the trouble to arrive early, and surely ought to be rewarded for this. Though perhaps the two ladies had arrived as early as they could? There was no knowing. But in any case there was an elementary justice in the first comers having the seats. The old lady would be perfectly all right in the corridor. The corridor was full of old ladies anyway, and no one else
45 seemed bothered by this, least of all the old ladies themselves! Dora hated pointless sacrifices. She was tired after her recent emotions and deserved rest. Besides, it would never do to arrive at her destination exhausted. She

– ece – in receive and similar words

regarded her state of distress as completely neurotic. She decided not to give up her seat.

50   She got up and said to the standing lady, 'Do sit down here, please. I'm not going very far, and I'd much rather stand anyway.'

'How very kind of you!' said the standing lady. 'Now I can sit next to my friend. I have a seat of my own further down, you know. Perhaps we can just exchange seats? Do let me help you to move your luggage.'

55   Dora glowed with delight. What is sweeter than the unhoped-for reward for the virtuous act?

She began to struggle along the corridor with the big suitcase, while the elderly lady followed with the canvas bag and Paul's hat. It was difficult to get along, and Paul's hat didn't seem to be doing too well. The train began
60 to move.

When they reached the other carriage it turned out that the lady had a corner seat by the window. Dora's cup was running over. The lady, who had very little luggage, departed and Dora was able to instal herself at once.

'Let me help you,' said a tall sunburnt man who was sitting opposite. He
65 hoisted the big case easily onto the rack, and Dora threw Paul's hat up after it. The man smiled in a friendly way. They sat down. Everyone in this carriage was thinner.

The Bell Iris Murdoch

Practice

(More than 1 hour)
Level: Full range 1 to 4

1 Give a broad outline, in 8 to 10 lines, of the incident.   (6)

2 What indications are there that Dora is unsure of herself?   (2)

3 Quote the phrase which shows that she had had an unpleasant time before getting on the train.   (1)

4 What thoughts go through her head after the second elderly lady enters (lines 23–49)?   (6)

5 Why does she feel uncomfortable?   (4)

6 How does the writer indicate the suddenness with which Dora changes her mind about giving up her seat?   (2)

7 What is the point of the last sentence?   (2)

8 What impressions do you get from this extract of Dora's:
a physical appearance?   (4)

b character?   (6)

                                           Total   (33)

Words state, but also imply.

Varieties of writing

Why we write

In order to write well, first decide what you want to say and then choose the best way of saying it; simple advice, but not so easy to follow, for to do so you need hours, months, even years of practice. But one thing is certain; the more you write and the more different types of writing you try the better you will become at it.

As with all aspects of English you must always keep a sense of audience in mind and identify the reasons and purposes for which you are writing.

Why then do you write?

MOTIVES	PURPOSES
because you have to	to express your feelings
as part of your job	to give an opinion
in school	to give information
in exams	to persuade
applying for job	to get something done
because you want to	
diaries	
personal letters	

Although the motives and purposes are separated here, they are in reality interconnected.

Practice

1 Can you think of any other motives and purposes for which people write?

2 Discuss briefly why the following people write:
a historian   a novelist   a copy writer in advertising   a sports reporter
a politician   a sign writer   the police in the course of their duty
pupils in school   exam candidates

3 Do you keep a diary? If you do, what type of entries do you make into it? If you knew it would be published what difference would it make to the matter you would put into it and the way you wrote?

Who is your audience?

Whatever you write in the course of school work or in exams will be read by a teacher or examiner. Outside school your audience will vary from yourself (e.g. as in diaries) to your friends and relations, to people unknown to you. You therefore need to practise writing with different audiences in mind and in different contexts or situations.

Different tasks require different types of writing.

Practice

1 Write out informal notes on the following.
   a You were going to prepare a light meal for your family (e.g. a salad), but finding you were short of food you have gone out to the shops. Explain what you have done, how you would like them to continue and how long you should be.
   b Your parents have gone out and should return at 10.00 p.m. You had told them you would be staying in, but friends phoned asking you to go round to their home. Explain in a note to your parents what has happened.

2 Write notes for the following.
   a You have bought a music centre which has quickly developed a number of faults. Ths shop where you bought it has asked you to return it giving all the necessary details.
   b You need to leave school early to pick up a younger brother, as the person who usually collects him is ill. The lesson you will miss is P.E. and you have missed it for the last three weeks for a variety of reasons.
   c Write instructions for someone who does not know how to use a piece of equipment which you have at home (e.g. washing machine).

There are two broad types of writing: expressive writing and writing directed for a practical purpose. The first may be referred to as writing in an open situation and includes narratives, essays, description; the second is a closed situation and includes reports, summaries, business letters.

Expressive writing

The different types of expressive writing do not fall into set categories of narrative, description argument, etc. For example, if you were asked to write on the topic 'Wet Sundays' you would probably include some description, some narrative and some thinking over or reflection in what you write. It is, therefore, probably better to think in terms of **techniques**, of the best way of giving an account, the different ways of describing effectively or of putting forward an argument. Nevertheless there will be some subjects which will be predominantly narrative or descriptive or persuasive.

Check carefully the punctuation of dialogue.

Structure

In all types of writing, structure is of the greatest importance. You should aim for the simple framework of:

1 a recognisable **opening**,
2 a **development section**,
3 a definite **conclusion**.

First, however you need to gather your material. If ideas are slow in coming it is often useful to write down the topic on a piece of paper and then jot down any ideas that it suggests. As you write down the ideas they, in turn, may suggest further ideas. For example, if you were asked to explore the main reasons for staying on after 16 in the same school or leaving to go to a Sixth Form or Tertiary College you might produce the following.

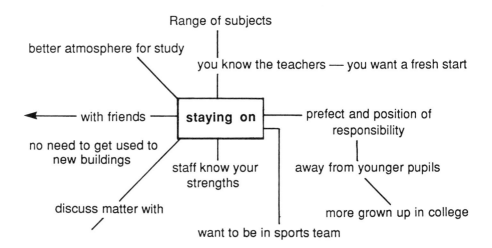

See how many of these lines of thought you can develop further. You now need to gather this material together and to put it into some form of order. The above material falls easily into two sections 'For' and 'Against'. You can organise it in another way by taking general topics and discussing the 'For and Against' in each topic, e.g. Staff, Subjects, Sport, Responsibilities. The diagram on page 88 shows how this sort of plan can be laid out.

Plan your writing and give it a structure.

This diagram gives at a glance the full structure of the topic.

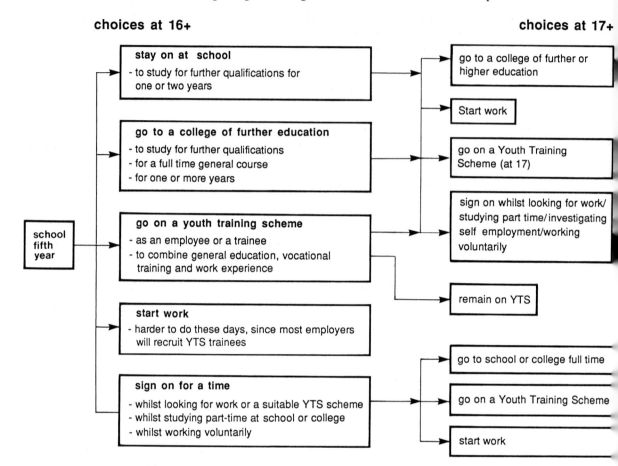

choices at 16+

choices at 17+

school fifth year

stay on at school
- to study for further qualifications for one or two years

go to a college of further or higher education

Start work

go to a college of further education
- to study for further qualifications
- for a full time general course
- for one or more years

go on a Youth Training Scheme (at 17)

sign on whilst looking for work/ studying part time/ investigating self employment/working voluntarily

go on a youth training scheme
- as an employee or a trainee
- to combine general education, vocational training and work experience

remain on YTS

start work
- harder to do these days, since most employers will recruit YTS trainees

go to school or college full time

sign on for a time
- whilst looking for work or a suitable YTS scheme
- whilst studying part-time at school or college
- whilst working voluntarily

go on a Youth Training Scheme

start work

Is there a structure in your writing?

Narrative writing

With narrative writing you tell a story or give an account of a series of events. The main emphasis has to be on the incidents or events so that the reader has a clear idea of what has happened. The simplest way of doing this is to:

1 begin at the beginning,
2 go on to what happens next,
3 describe the outcome.

Other techniques are also used, such as the flashback.

The most difficult part of narrative writing is often the **opening**. Some writers like a dramatic, gripping opening, e.g.

'As I turned round and saw her point the gun at me I knew I had made a mistake, a deadly mistake, I thought.'

The difficulty with this type of writing lies in keeping up the excitement and level of interest as the story **develops**. You should not crowd your narrative with too many incidents, but pace them out so that the level of interest is maintained. Note the importance of background and characters in well developed stories. The **ending** should round off the story giving a satisfactory conclusion. Some writers like to leave their readers in the air at the end, but this can be a very difficult type of ending to achieve. It is like having a mystery story without telling the reader at the end who did it.

Points to watch

1 Do you tell the story in the first person (i.e. **I**) or in the third person (i.e. **she, he**)? Both have advantages and difficulties. Try working out what they are.

2 As verbs carry the action along, vary them, particularly those which refer to movement e.g. **plodded**, **trudged**, **stumbled**, **darted**.

3 If you use dialogue vary the verbs of saying. A thesaurus will help you.

4 If verbs are important so therefore are adverbs, which should be chosen carefully.

5 The tenses of the verbs need careful attention. Do not switch from the past to the present unless for a particular effect.

6 Avoid repeating **then** too often.

Then, and then, and then, and then . . .

Practice

1 Study the following as a start to a story and then make up similar starts for P.E., Biology, R.E., and Home Economics lessons.

'I have enough gunpowder in this jar to blow up this school,' said Miss Lockhart in even tones. . . . The extreme hush that fell was only what she expected, for she always opened the first science lesson with those words and with the gunpowder in front of her.

The Prime of Miss Jean Brodie

2 Think up opening paragraphs which catch the reader's attention for:
a A Night in the Waxworks
b The Happiest Day of My Life

3 Write out the outline of a story for which the following is the opening.

The body of the supermarket manager had been taken away from his office; the police photographer had finished but the rest of the police team still had work to do. Detective Chief Inspector Hardy looked at the five people standing in a group behind the door. One of them, he was certain, was the murderer, but before he spoke to them he thought of what the doctor had said: 'A blow on the head, but there is a strange smell from his mouth'.

4 The following is the opening of a space fiction story. It contains the seeds of the rest of the story.
a Write down what information is given.
b Complete the story.

Cosmoprobe IV was preparing to enter Area B which was the final stage before entering Galactic Time. The move from Accelerated Time to Galactic Time was a very difficult and dangerous manoeuvre. Even a micro-second delay would destroy the vast cosmocraft immediately. It would simply cease to exist. Every personum in the crew had a particular job to do and even the space explorers had a task. While the manoeuvre was being made there had to be total silence. The speech contact in each personum was therefore cut off. The critical micro-second for re-entry was successfully passed, but within .5 of a micro-second the cosmocraft lurched violently sideways and then within a milli-second came back on course. The panel in front of the Flight Commander showed that the personum at Port 7 had been .1 of a milli-second late in its contact. The Flight Commander frowned. When the captives from Helion had been re-constituted into persona they were also programmed for .001 milli-second response. Could it be that one . . .? Before he could finish the question a harsh, violet light filled the Command Room. It meant that they were coming back on a different – and unidentified – time beam from the one that they had left earth on. Having been de-emotionalized, he could not panic, but he fully realised what the consequences could be.

Slang – only in dialogue

Descriptive writing

Observation

To describe well you first need to observe well. A good writer sees what other people do not see and has the words to express it in such a way that they can see it. You can train yourself to be observant. You tend to notice first those things that affect your **senses**. Many people can remember vividly smells and tastes, particularly unpleasant ones, from their childhood. The sense of sight, however, can become dulled and you can be so used to looking at familiar sights that you fail to notice the variety in them.

Practice

1 Look at a room that you think is not particularly interesting, e.g. a classroom or a room at home. Write down a list of:
   a the colours and shades of colour in it,
   b the noises and sounds,
   c the shape of the objects,
   d the feel of different objects.
   It will be surprising if you have fewer than twenty items on your list and these can form the basis of a good description.

2 Which of the senses do you associate with the following? Write down the words which apply to them.
   a dentist's room,   d school dining room,
   b vet's waiting room,   e chemistry laboratory,
   c farmyard,   f P.E. changing room.

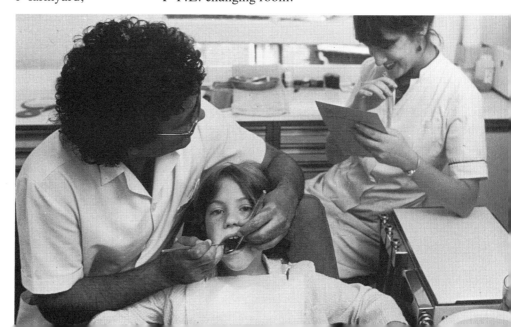

Feelings

Feelings are closely connected with the senses. If you can describe the way you or other people involved react to the scene or person or event, then this can make your writing more realistic. It is, however, more difficult than a straight forward description of colour, sounds, etc. You may need to use such abstract nouns as fear, warmth, anxiety, happiness, but your writing will be more effective if you vary physical description with feeling and if the feeling can be conveyed in a direct way, e.g. the extract on Adolf (page 28).

Practice

1 To the list of words which you have written for question **1** on page 91 describe the feelings you would have in the situations given.

2 Describe briefly the feelings you would find in the following:
   a a children's ward in a hospital on Christmas Day,
   b a road accident,
   c a shy boy asking a girl to go out with him,
   d waiting for exam results,
   e an appeal for famine victims.

Detail

Detail is an important element of good description. Again, this depends on good observation. By focusing on a small part you can bring the reader very close to the scene or person being described. For example, in a brochure for a Fun Park they talk about the 'whiteknuckle rides'. What vivid sensations does this suggest and is the focus only on the knuckles? Most scenes, places or people have at least one striking quality, one prominent feature which attracts attention immediately. It may be the drabness, the variety of colour, the peacefulness, the buzz and activity, beautiful eyes or a large nose. Making this the centre of your description and building up around it can be very effective. If you exaggerate prominent features out of proportion with the rest you produce a caricature, such as cartoonists often draw. Many writers use this technique and it is worth studying and imitating. Two examples from Dickens show how it can be done.

Uriah Heep in *David Copperfield*

Hardly any eyebrows, and no eyelashes, and eyes of a red-brown, so unsheltered and unshaded that I remember wondering how he went to sleep. He was high-shouldered and bony and had a long, lank, skeleton hand which particularly attracted my attention. It was not fancy of mine about his hands, I observed, for he frequently ground the palms against each other as if to squeeze them dry and warm, besides often wiping them in a stealthy way on his pocket handkerchief.

[His eyes, boniness and hands are at the centre of this description.]

Have you strayed off the subject?

Miss Haversham in *Great Expectations*

She was dressed in rich materials – satins, and lace, and silks – all in white.
Her shoes were white, and she had a long white veil dependant from her hair,
but her hair was white. Some bright jewels sparkled on her neck and on her
hands. I saw that everything within my view which ought to be white had been
white long ago, and had lost its lustre, and was faded and yellow. I saw that
the bride within the bridal dress had withered like the dress, and like the
flowers, and had no brightness left but the brightness of her sunken eyes.

Practice

1 List what you think the prominent features of the following are and try to
describe them in the manner above.
a circus clown,
b well known pop singer,
c teacher,
d shopping centre on a Sunday morning,
e industrial scene in wet weather.

Overall description

Detail, however, should not be described for its own sake. It should add to the
overall description. Films often focus on detail and then suddenly widen to
take in the full scene. The reverse, i.e. starting with the panoramic view and
then fixing onto a detail, is also often used. Both techniques can be effective in
written description and you should try both. Another cinematic technique is
panning across a scene, as a cine-camera does as it films from one side to the
other. The following opening to a book includes an appeal to the senses, detail
and an overall view of the scene.

The airport was hot and stuffy. Five flights had been delayed and consequently
there were twice as many people in it as it had been built for. The big, bulky
man sitting near to the windows overlooking the runway was obviously
uncomfortable in a suit and collar and tie. The sweat was running down his
forehead onto his dark thick eyebrows and from there round the scar at the
side of his cheek. The loudspeaker announced the arrival of a flight from
Athens. The bulky man immediately stood up and went out onto the walkway.
In the intense heat the runway shimmered like the surface of a lake. He caught
sight of the aircraft on his right as it slowly lowered itself; his eyes followed it
along the length of the runway to the point on his extreme left where it came to
a halt. Two hundred metres further on, the van and truck were in place.
All was going as planned.

Do the paragraphs follow on naturally?

Adjectives   Good descriptive writing often depends on accurate choice of adjectives. Try to put the following into practice.

1 Do not over use adjectives. This is a fault commonly found in journalism. Many reporters do not like using a noun without an adjective in front of it.

2 Avoid unnecessary adjectives as in:

past history
grateful thanks
free gifts

3 Avoid also groups of adjectives in threes as they are often clichés:

tall, dark and handsome
cool, calm and collected
fair, fat and forty

4 Make the adjectives work for you. There are many adjectives in the two passages by Dickens, but they all have a job to do and do it well.

5 Remember the rules of comparison:
  a The suffix – **er** or 'more' is used with the adjective if you are comparing two items, e.g. John is taller and more handsome than his brother.
  b The suffix – **est** or 'most' is used with the adjective when you are comparing more than two, e.g. Jane is the tallest and most beautiful girl in her form.

6 Some adjectives are absolute, that is, they should not be modified in the above manner, e.g. a **more** or **most** nuclear war does not make sense. Other examples of absolute adjectives are **unique, entire, perfect, total, complete.**

Good practice guide – descriptive writing

1 Appeal to the senses and feelings.

2 Use physical details to indicate character.

3 Clothes are often a guide to character.

4 Take care with the use of adjectives.

5 Balance between the use of detail and overall description.

6 Note cinematic techniques and try to use them.

Check the use of the apostrophe, page 154.

Argumentative writing

Discussion or argumentative writing puts forwards a point of view in order to persuade the reader. More than any other type of writing, it needs good planning and clear cut structure. The simplest way of doing this is to draw two columns, head one 'For' and the other 'Against' and beneath each heading put down as many points as you can think of.

Are Holidays Abroad Worthwhile?

For
Against

Conclusion

A slight variation of this is to state your opinion at the start and then argue for and against from there.

However, although this will do, such essays tend to lack sparkle and be uninteresting. A better, but more difficult way, is to select four or five main ideas and then work out supporting arguments or extensions to them (see page 88).

Paragraphing

Paragraphing is very important in this type of writing. Good paragraphing forms the main structure. Each paragraph should be on one topic or on a topic with extensions to it. If you start writing a discussion essay without a plan you will almost certainly repeat yourself, particularly if you are short of ideas. Even a very general plan will help you to avoid this.

Holidays Abroad

Paragraph 1   Introduction; cold, wet winter's night
Paragraph 2   Excitement of planning
Paragraph 3   Excitement of travel
Paragraph 4   Cost of holidays abroad
Paragraph 5   Scenery
Paragraph 6   Good weather and facilities
Paragraph 7   Foreign customs and food
Paragraph 8   Conclusion

With dialogue, vary the verbs of saying.

The order of paragraphs given is not the best, but with one or two changes you can produce a plan in which each paragraph leads on naturally to the next. Note that the plan does not indicate whether you are in favour or not of holidays abroad, but allows you to develop arguments for and against in each paragraph. Another point to watch is the use of signpost words (see page 27), that is words which develop, emphasise or change the course of the discussion, e.g.

development: and, also, in addition, furthermore, next, eventually.
emphasis: in particular, particularly, especially, moreover, in fact, in reality, indeed.
alternative: but, however, on the other hand, in contrast, on the contrary, whereas, against this.

Practice

1 Write out the main ideas, in any order, for the following and then construct an orderly plan for them.
   a Should the death penalty be re-introduced?
   b All youths below the age of twenty years should have to do one year's community service.
   c If I had the power, the laws I would introduce.
   d Television is a greater influence for good than for bad.
   e The biggest danger to the future is . . .
   f Science Fiction is fairy tales with micro-electronics in them.

Good practice guide – argumentative writing

1 Indentify the topic and make certain you have a clear idea of what is required.

2 Underline the important words in the title.

3 You may have an opinion about the topic, but do you have sufficient knowledge or facts to sustain a well developed argument?

5 As you are writing, check that you are keeping to the topic and have not changed it e.g. from **Holidays Abroad** to **A Holiday Abroad**.

6 Use paragraphing to develop your argument.

7 One paragraph – one main idea – supporting ideas – examples.

8 Use signpost words to develop, emphasise and conclude your arguments.

One paragraph – one main topic

Writing to explain

Explanatory (or **expository** writing) is a type of descriptive writing, for you are describing a process of how something works. The topic may be quite broad, e.g. 'Explain the educational system in England and Wales' to something much narrower. To find out the most important aspect of this type of writing, imagine you were lost in a town centre and you asked someone how to get to the bus station. For the answer to be helpful what would it have to be? You would need to be given the correct order of directions and the words would have to be precise, leaving no room for misunderstanding.

The order of giving the information is important. It should be clear-cut and progress from one stage to the next. A plan is important (see pages 87 and 88). If the order is not clear in your mind it will be less clear on the page. Remember the purpose of this writing is to explain to the reader and it will be judged on its success in doing so.

The accuracy of the language is the second point. If you have to use technical expressions you will have to judge which of them need explaining. There is a tendency to use imperatives – **do this**, **do that** – or indirect imperatives – **you should do this**, **you should do that** (as is used in this book). As this writing is also concerned mainly with facts, the result may be dry and abrupt sounding. Try to soften this. As sequencing is important vary the words which convey progression (see page 97). Over use of **then**, **and then** can be monotonous. Finally, here is an example of a piece of tongue-in-cheek explanatory writing by a writer of humorous verse and books. It not only pokes fun at this type of writing, but illustrates its techniques as well.

To make Gosky Patties

Take a Pig, three or four years of age, and tie him by the off-hind leg to a post. Place five pounds of currants, three of sugar, two pecks of peas, eighteen roast chest-nuts, a candle, and six bushels of turnips, within his reach; if he eats these, constantly provide him with more.

Then procure some cream, some slices of Cheshire cheese, four quires of foolscap paper, and a packet of black pins. Work the whole into a paste and spread it out to dry on a sheet of clean brown water-proof linen.

When the paste is perfectly dry, but not before, proceed to beat the Pig violently, with the handle of a large broom. If he squeals, beat him again.

Visit the paste and beat the Pig alternately for some days, and ascertain if at the end of that period the whole is about to turn into Gosky Patties.

If it does not then, it never will; and in that case the Pig may be let loose, and the whole process may be considered as finished.

Edward Lear

Language to suit your purpose and audience

Practice

1 On page 88 information is given in diagrammatic form as a plan for a discussion essay. Use the same information for an article explaining the options open to you for further education.

2 Imitating the style and approach of the recipe by Edward Lear on page 98, explain the way the following nonsense schemes could be put into operation:
   a Making dehydrated water cubes to be stored for times of drought.
   b Extracting sunbeams from flowers and storing them for wintry days.

3 Make an outline plan or first draft for:
   a the development of the Woman's Movement,
   b aspects of racism,
   c organising a camping holiday,
   d the national provision of leisure facilities,
   e the curriculum offered in your school.

Good practice guide – writing for explanation

1 Sort out in your mind the order.

2 Make a plan.

3 Check that each stage progresses naturally to the next.

4 Vocabulary has to be precise.

5 Explain technical terms, but do not use too many of them.

6 Avoid repeating **then**, **and then**.

Do not repeat 'then' too often.

Writing tasks

Mainly narrative
1 The Holiday that Went Wrong.

2 Tell a story about an occasion when you made a very embarrassing mistake.

3 Give an account of an accident or emergency you were involved in.

4 The Day I Hit the Jackpot.

5 Give an account of a day or evening when you had to look after a younger brother or sister.

6 The Interview.

7 The Best Party I Have Ever Been To.

8 On pages 104 and 105 there is a strip cartoon of two television comedians, Cannon and Ball. Write out the incident as a story including all the dialogue in the cartoon. You will also have to provide some description and narrative links between the frames of the cartoon.

9 On pages 106, 107 and 108 there is a photo-story. Write it out as narrative with the appropriate dialogue, descriptions and narrative links.

Write a narrative account of the events leading up to this accident. ▶

Do not use too many technical terms.

Use the pictures to compose a narrative. If the sequence of pictures was b, a, c, what different narrative could you write?

a

b

c

Use these photos and the advert on page 113 as material for a narrative or discussion.

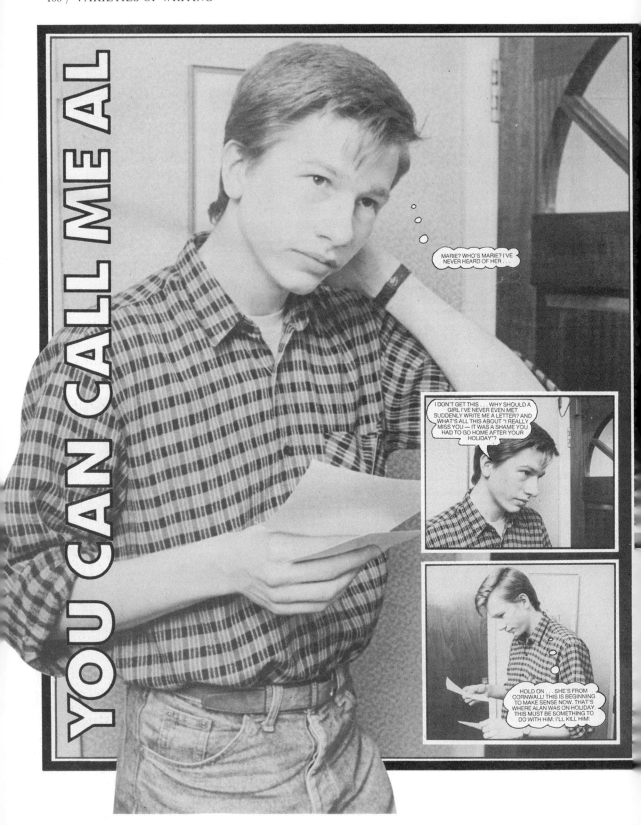

CONTINUED ON PAGE 33

Personal experience

1 Write about your memories of the games you played in childhood. Describe the games, how they were played and the attitudes of the people playing them. Include any other aspects which make them particularly memorable.

2 Some pets I know, and their owners.

3 Describe two or three toys (including dolls, teddies) that you have kept from childhood and say why you have kept them.

4 You often hear older people talk of the 'Good Old Days'. What parts of present day life do you think you will look back at with affection in later years?

5 In what ways have you changed in the last five years? Try to assess whether the change has been for the better.

6 A person from your town has become famous and on a return visit criticises it in the local paper. Imagine what such criticism could be and write a reply.

7 The Best Film I Have Seen.

Descriptive and reflective

1 Wet Sundays.

2 Describe two or three walks near your home which would be of interest to outsiders.

3 Describe two contrasting buildings, one of historical interest and the other very modern in design. Say what attracts, or does not attract you, to them.

4 What do you think is a good job? Consider not only pay, but working conditions, prospects, interest and any other points you think appropriate. Look at two or three jobs from this point of view and say which would suit you.

5 A time in the past you would have liked to live in and why.

6 The difference between living in England and in . . . .

7 Describe a fireworks display or a carnival procession or a village festival you have attended. Include the build up to the activity.

8 Describe three well known people who are in different occupations. Give a description of their character as well as their appearance and say what you think about them.

9 The Humorous Side of School Life.

10 My Kind of Music.

11 Dangerous Occupations I Could or Could Not Do.

12 An Out-Patients or Casualty Department of a Hospital.

Good description needs good observation

This woman is reflecting on her life. ▶
Write an account of her thoughts and feelings.

Same woman,
two hairstyles:
describe the difference.

Describe the two scenes to bring out the qualities and feelings of each.

Argument and discussion

1 Why do you think soap operas are so popular on television? Refer to at least three in your answer.

2 It is said that children grow up more quickly these days. If this is so, do you think they should be allowed to start full time work at 14 years of age? Try to consider all the implications of this.

3 Discuss the ways women are presented in advertising. Use examples from television, newspapers, magazines and consider two or three in detail.

Is there a structure in your writing?

4 'You can't be a full time student if you have a part time job.' Do you agree?

5 'For me, the greatest problem facing British society in the near future is . . .'

6 Do you think boys and girls should be taught the same subjects and in the same classes from 11–16 years?

7 Construct and describe what you would think to be a well-balanced evening's viewing on television from 5.00 p.m. to 10.00 p.m.

8 'We attach too much importance to sport and furthermore most sports people are overpaid.' Do you agree?

9 What do you think are the problems which people living in the inner city face? Have you any suggestions how they may be overcome?

10 'I have a house, a husband and four children to look after so I haven't time to get a job.' Discuss the implications of this statement.

11 Overpaid and Underpaid Occupations.

12 Do you think we are too soft with criminals?

13 Why do you think there has been a great increase in drug taking and what can be done about it?

14 Discuss three or four advances in technology which can be used either for good or for bad purposes.

15 Do a survey of teenage magazines and the purposes they serve.

16 Do you think 'Agony Aunts' serve a useful purpose either in magazines or phone-in programmes? Discuss why people write to them, why the magazines provide them and give examples to back up your opinions.

17 Why is there so much interest in horoscopes? Do you believe that people do conform to the categories of their birth sign? Give examples from your own experience.

Problem solving and imaginative

1 What do you think would happen if suddenly on one day the world ran out of petrol and oil?

2 Suppose you woke one morning to find that you had turned bright green. Imagine what the day would be like, how people would react to you and how you would cope.

3 Give an account or short story of what would happen if all circles suddenly became square.

4 Suggest improvements that could be made to the human body.

5 Give your ideas on ways to solve the following problems. Include sketches if you think them appropriate.
   a How to get wheelchair-bound people down in safety from the top floors of a department store in the event of a fire. Lifts are not to be used and outside ramps may be cut off by the fire.
   b Some gadgets to help a person with no use in the arms to get through a normal day.

6 Alongside are items from different newspapers on one day. Imagine you were a TV news editor and had to provide a script for a twenty minute news broadcast. Study the items, decide the order in which they are to appear and write out the script.

7 'That day, that dreadful day, when I looked into the mirror and raised my left arm, the image in the mirror raised its right; when I smiled, the image frowned.' Continue the story.

8 Draw up a report with diagrams, if necessary, which discusses:
   a whether two drinks dispensers, two snacks dispensers and a space invader machine should be allowed in school, and
   b the best place to site them if they are allowed.

9 Imagine you were in charge of a firm which planned to introduce a pizzaburger or miniburger on a trial basis.
   a Draw up a report which includes a description of the product, reasons for introducing it, the likely market for it, four or five places where it could be tried out.
   b Either design or describe the publicity material that you would recommend.

Are you repeating yourself?

The champs!

Soccer friendly off as team arrested

Doctors divided over the patient's right to know

Army goes in search of Incas and edible frogs

Concorde close to mid-air disaster

Living man is heart donor

New hopes for peace as Arab rivals meet

Let 16-year-olds have the vote says law group

One paragraph – one main topic

A selection of essays follows. Essay One received a Grade A; Essay Two received a Grade F. Study both of them and list the reasons why you think they received the grades they did. Read the remaining essays and give each the grade you think it deserves. Use either the Assessment Guide on page 117 or the following mark scheme.

Subject matter   **30%**
How interesting, relevant is it?
Does it explore thoroughly the topic given?

Construction   **20%**
Is there an order and structure to the writing? Does it progress naturally
and logically bringing out not only wider matters, but also details?

Vocabulary and language   **20%**
variety and breadth in use, appropriate to the purpose and audience

Mechanical accuracy   **20%**
in grammar and punctuation

Spelling   **10%**

Has the narrative a beginning, middle and end?

Assessment guide – varieties of writing

The following are broad guidelines for assessing the level of achievement in your own writing and that of others. As the way we write varies according to the nature and purpose of what we write, then the guidelines will refer to some types of writing, but not necessarily to others. For example,

▣ 1 = A/B
▣ 2 = C/D
▣ 3 = D/E
▣ 4 = F/G

'Ability to control the development of a story line' will not apply to a discussion essay.

The levels 1 to 4 are roughly equivalent to the GCSE grades as shown left.

Level 4
1 Covers some of the topic
2 Can recognise and convey broad outlines of character, opinions and information
3 Can reorganise main items of information
4 Shows some sense of audience
5 Some use of paragraphing is evident
6 Simple vocabulary and sentence structure
7 Spelling and punctuation are good enough not to cause difficulty in understanding

Level 3
8 Can gather information, select from it and reproduce it in mainly own words
9 Can control simple narrative techniques and characterisation where appropriate
10 Can recognise and represent different points of view
11 There is a clear structure to the writing with paragraphs of an appropriate length
12 Shows a wider range of vocabulary and can recognise the connection between choice of words and effect
13 Spelling and punctuation allow the meaning to be understood easily

Level 2
14 Wider ranging treatment of the topic
15 Can make judgement based on material given and summarise it
16 Can develop an argument coherently
17 Can control dialogue, characters, storyline, feeling and description with the reader in mind
18 Paragraphing is consistent with the development of the topic
19 Variety in choice of words and sentence structure consistent with the nature and purpose of the writing
20 More difficult punctuation marks used consistently

Level 1
21 Thorough exploration of the topic, at different levels where necessary
22 Wide variety in the use of words and sentence structure
23 Full control of the language used as a means of creating character, narrative, feelings, arguments consistent with audience and purpose of the writing
24 Spelling and punctuation are consistently correct

Essay one

The following is an example of a piece of writing that was given Grade A. It does not mean that there are no mistakes in it. Faults that were mentioned included:

careless mistakes, e.g. **where** for **were**
too chatty in tone including slang and colloquialisms

However, it was given an 'A'. What qualities does it have which you think make it worth an 'A'?

Fire

It must have been smouldering for hours, for when it finally came into blaze it was late afternoon. The enquiry which was held later established that it had started in a room which had been empty for some time and in which a lot of rubbish had accumulated. Evidently people used to go in there to have their
5   sandwiches at the lunch break. They weren't supposed to, but they did and probably one of them dropped a cigarette butt. One small match or cigarette brought down a complete building and put more than 50 people out of a job, besides the two fatalities and other injuries.

I know what happened because my brother worked there on a Y.T.S.
10   Scheme. The building was a very old, disused warehouse which had been empty for many years. All of us used to play hide and seek and spooks in there, when we were kids. We used to go in by the broken windows. But after a serious accident to a toddler all the glass and windows were boarded up. Then an enterprise scheme took it over and each of the six floors was turned
15   into a small business. My brother used to assemble and pack fancy goods.

The first I knew was when I heard a fire alarm. I took no notice because they were always going off in the old ramshackle buildings around us. Alan told me that it had started on the floor above where he worked. One of the girls was going to the loo when she saw smoke coming from under the door.
20   Like most of us would, she opened it and a huge cloud of smoke rushed out. She didn't panic but rushed back to the work room yelling 'Fire! Fire!' Nobody of course took any notice of her, thinking it was one of the jokes they all used to play on each other. But when they smelled the smoke they got out. One of them tried the fire alarm on their floor, but it didn't work. Unfortunately,
25   Sharon had left the door open creating a draft which fanned the smouldering rubbish into flames. They were not going to be caged in a little room, but rushed out with a roar looking out for any dry material which they could catch hold of. And there was plenty of that.

Alan got a whiff of the smoke as the people from the job above came
30   bellowing down the narrow stairs. He had the presence of mind to smash the glass on the fire alarm and this time it worked.

This is what I heard at home. A few minutes later my mum said, "I'm sure I can smell smoke outside" I went out with her, she was right It was about four o'clock and already quite dark. Suddenly we saw a faint, orangey glow
35   in the darkness and then we heard the awful screech of the fire engines with their alarms blaring away. Then the glow changed into a vivid bright orange and there were huge bangs or explosions. The sky was lit up like a firework

Do not repeat 'then' too often.

display and there were hundreds, thousands of brilliant sparks like stars against the blackness of the night.

40 'That's somewhere near Alan's place' my mum said.'

'Yes' I said and as I said it we looked at each other aghast, our eyes and mouths open wide. We didn't say anything else, but shot off leaving the door of the house open. The warehouse was about half a mile away and we must have broken the British record. Thank goodness when we got there the first

45 person we saw was Alan. My mum grabbed hold of him and hugged him and was starting to cry I think when he said that there were at least four people missing. The whole building was now ablaze. Huge, thrusting tongues of fire where coming out from where the windows and doors had been. I could not believe that such a big building, old though it was, could go up so quickly.

50 There were more explosions, the glass in the windows probably, but no, evidently there was a paint store on the fifth floor and the flames had greedily reached it.

The heat was intense and it was now dangerous to be near the warehouse. The police and firemen started to push people further back but most were

55 reluctant to move. They stood there with a mixture of awe, fear fascination on their faces. Some were enjoying it. Others had started the usual rumours 'I've heard there's still ten left in there'. 'They've no chance now, they've had it' 'I heard the inspector say there's fifteen missing' A neighbour of ours, Mrs. O'Rourke suddenly screamed out that her husband was working in there and

60 she couldn't find him. A policewoman immediately took her away to her boss who was trying to account for everyone who should have been in the building. Because of the heat the firemen could not get in close. They now had six engines there and from the top of their tall ladders they were pumping hundreds of gallons of water into the seething inferno. But they might as well

65 have been throwing bucketsful of water at it.

The flames went up quickly, but the blaze and smoke died down slowly. It was still smouldering the following day and we had the taste of smoke in our mouths for ages afterwards. Two people died in the fire. Mr. O'Rourke was not one of them. He had sneaked out from work with a mate to go to a pub.

70 But what happened to him afterwards is another story.

Time taken: 1 hr 15 mins

With dialogue, vary the verbs of saying.

Essay two

One day we decided to go to Italy for are hoiladay's.

Then we decided to go by car because we couldn't get the day we wanted to fly ~~buy~~ by plane.

It was friday morning, we got up about 9 o'clock.

We had are breakfast, we went shopping then we packed the car and we ~~sat~~ our lunch and clean up.

We put water and dog food in the dog's dishe's, we feed the fish and then we left the house and got into the car.

We all got into the car, we waved our neighbour's goodbye and off we went.

We stopped at the petrol station and ~~fills~~ filled her up with petrol.

Then ~~of off~~ we went to the motorway, we looked out for the sign's heading towards Dover the shipport were we loaded on the ship.

It took us 8 hur's to get ~~their~~ there because we stopped to fill the car up and to eat, rest and refresh our-selve's.

Then when we arrived at Dover, we were 2 hur's early, so went went into this big masive sort of shopping centre, we eat and drank and refreshed are selve's-up, put clean clothes on and then we had to load on the ship because the called on the radio-speaker's "Dover to Ostend boarding now please!"

"Dover to Ostend please!"

Was we or were we?

So we got to our car and drove up the isle and then we waited about 15 minute's in the car before we could get out and we had to wait for the over driver's and passenger's ~~too to~~ to board.

Then we got out and went up the stair's to the sitting room and sat down.

I fell asleep because I was tierd.

I woke up and it was ready to get off the ship.

But the weather was nice.

The sea was very ~~carm~~ calm and it was a good safe journey.

Then he went down the stairs and we got into our car's drove of and then we were in Beligum.

Then we went straight on , through Beligum and we arrived in germany about 800 o'clock in the evening. It was about 6.45 p.m. in England.

Then we had to rest in this bed break-fast place called Trotter's bar.

It was ~~a~~ a lovely big sort of hôtel attbined with bar and dinner (resturant).

Then we had our dinner and went to bed.

We woke up about 800 o'clock and had are break-fast and then set of again.

We looked for the sign's heading out of Germany into Austria.

We then got out of Germany about 10.00° clock and the stayed in an-other bed-break-fast place.

We had our tea and went to bed.

But I just couldn't sleep, I kept on

Check the use of the apostrophe, page 154.

thinking how far apart I am from my
family back in England.
I turned round to ask my sister if she
was missing good old England but she was
asleep.
She was ~~snoring~~ snoring her head of and the I
just lay there there thinking and fell asle
Morning came and I couldn't get up I was
so tired but I had to because I was not
far from my gran's, about 10 hur.
I got up flung on my track-suit and went
for a jog before my break-fast.
Then got back and had my break-fast.

Then we got in the car and looked for the
sign's heading for Austria but going
toward's Italy, we arrived in Italy,
about 400°clock p.m.

Essay three

Young people today often feel that they don't have enough freedom. How far do you think it is true?

To be free to have no cares. Doing what you want, when you want, how you want, it would seem bliss to some young people. No longer having the alarm clock schreeching down your ears at 7 o'clock in the morning. telling you to get out of bed and go to school. No teachers bellowing at you if you forget
5 your homework. No adults ordering you down from your bedroom to do the washing up when you are listening to your favourite records. Just having the ability to run your own life, to have freedom. Freedom, the condition of not being in the power of another. Being unrestricted or independant seems a very tempting prospect to many young people who feel they do not have enough
10 in today's world.

But no-one has total freedom, not even tyrants or dictators who are still governed by the rest of the world. If everyone had total freedom there would be chaos, no law and order. It would be a very dangerous world, people could go around killing one another quite freely.
15 Some young people think that they do not have enough freedom because of jobs or tasks they have to do. They do not like others having authority over them. But they forget, the people who have this authority like teachers, parents etc. are older, have seen more of the world and are more experienced than their jumniors, and even these people do not have freedom. They have
20 to obey their bosses, whom have to obey their bosses and so it works up, everyone pushed into their position. The law has to be obeyed by everyone, no matter what age, race or gender. Young people have to learn from and respect their elders and so one day they will hopefully be responsible people with authority over others. Not power though no one likes someone having
25 power over them. Power, the ability to compel obedience out of fear is quite different from authority, the ability to make someone obey because understand and respect, not necessarily agree with the reasons.

And in today's world youngsters have a lot of freedom. They might complain because they have to go to school, wear a uniform, do jobs or help around
30 the house but there are always reasons for these things. And, in the past children had very little freedom. Children had to be seen but not heard, to speak only when spoken to and to have great honour and respect for their parents and their parent's wishes. Children, then, were like ornaments pushed in a cupboard and only brought out on special occasions.
35 School is one item where young people feel they do not have enough freedom. Why wear a horrible, dreary, boring uniform that's so unfashionable and makes you look like everyone else? What difference does a uniform make? After all, teachers wear what they want. But if pupils wore their own clothes there would be great competition in class, as to who was most fashionable, and
40 insensible clothes would be worn. And what about pupils whose parents could not afford to clothe them in such fashions? At least with a school uniform everyone looks the same. Uniform also gives merit and distinction. Another quibble is the homework and the amount given. It is felt that too much is given, there is no time to go out in the evenings, holidays seem full of work.

Are you writing to the topic?

45 This is often true but if homework is done as it is received and is started early in the evening the load can be lessened. And homework is necessary, for teachers to see how we work by ourselves and also because there are not enough school hours for all the work to be done in.

Young people don't like the hold teachers have on them making them do 50 homework, giving detentions, reprimanding them for being late etc. But someone has a hold over the teachers – heads of department, headmaster, education committee, minister of education and so. Just like the pupils, the teachers too have to buckle down.

In society, out of school, young people feel there is a lack of freedom for 55 them. They try to blame their crimes on this,

'Well, there's nowhere to go, nothing to do. That's why we graffitied on that wall.' or

'What else was there to do? Mugging an old lady was a distraction.'

Often there are a lack of facilities, no youth clubs, sports centres or cinemas, 60 but other amusements can be found. How about doing an old lady's shopping instead of mugging her or putting artistic talent into pictures?

Young people don't like the rules that govern society. They feel banned, trapped, a vendetta against them. Not allowed to smoke under 16, buy alcohol under 18, films at the cinema are rated and you cannot get in.

65 Chores at home restrict young people – washing up, tidying rooms, looking after the baby. Why should they do this? After all, it was not their fault that their parents decided to have another baby. Why should parents have authority over them? Again, the answer is the same. Everyone has a position, things to do and the people who have authority over you also have people who have 70 authority over them. If young people thought a bit more about others and not just themselves they would see that they are not the only ones without freedom.

Everyone as a child, and future generations too, was or will be subject to these rules. But even so you grow older, as some rules disappear more come 75 in their places showing that everyone, not just young people, do not have freedom.

Where is place; were the plural of was

Essay Four

I was afraid and I had to pray and say 'O God, you made the storm, preserve my people.'

My praying was very hypocritical, a plea to a God I had rejected and abandoned long ago. Life has been harsh to me, I have received my fare share of suffering but I have come through it all. I have survived, though I am crushed and broken. Here I am now, with unwanted responsibility for a rag-tag group of losers and drop-outs, the very dregs of society which I professed to despise. The scorn with which I held them had melted away into pity, what a fool I was allowing weak emotions to inspire my involvement with this motley crew.

So there we were, hopeless and homeless, shivering by a pier awaiting a ship that never came, nor never would, in a howling storm. How my so called friends would laugh to see me now; how fallen are the mighty! I, who once commanded respect, am now looked upon with disdain. The wealth that I and my family did possess is all gone either squandered by my compulsive gambler of a brother or stolen by a so-called friend.

Marie de Vaicalle is my name, and I speak it with pride. I am the last living member of a once powerful family. Such is the tragedy of their deaths, but it is one of many, noble families murdered by the rabblement on the streets and their commanding faction in this bloody massacre they call a revolution. The guillotine will always haunt me, perhaps that is my fated doom. Gone is the splendour that once was France, all that is left is this miserable hell-hole.

My name is pseunonymous with traitor, but is is not I, but them who betrayed the king; theirs is the treason not mine, ungrateful dogs that they are. I am a symbol for their uncontained hate, one of the last survivors of the aristocracy who must be eliminated and my death a public spectacle.

I saw my family hacked to death by an insane mob, my father was butchered before my very eyes and I watched as my tortured brother writhed in pain from their barbaric obsceneties. Is it any wonder I am bitter and twisted and bent on revenge, or that I am sly and devious when I have seen the inhuman horrors committed, the nightmare which will never leave me? The only thing I crave before I die is to kill the man who betrayed my family's whereabouts to their murderers. I vow that he shall suffer as they did.

I am cynical. There is no warm emotion within me, only cold, cruel thoughts, or so I believed. But on witnessing this group of mis-fits, some mamed by the atrocities of these lunatics, that I was moved to pity. Something I have not felt for so long. I have nurtured my hate, fed it with bitterness and seen it grow, and directed it at all the lower classes. But I was enlightened. It was not only I that suffered, some were hurt more than me, and for this I felt ashamed. I wanted to make amends to the maltreated and physically wounded. By leading this pathetic group of people to a ship that would take them to England, I felt I would achieve that aim. It never arrived. I should have known not to trust anybody except myself, I have failed them and for this I cannot forgive myself.

I can see the torches and her the shouts of the crowd, but I do not care. I shall not run nor give them the satisfaction of them seeing I am afraid. I shall accept my fate, and nobody shall grieve me, for I am just another aristocrat condemned to the terrors of the French Revolution.   Time: 1 hr

---

Has the narrative a beginning, middle and end?

Essay Five

After the warm air of the party inside, the man was relieved to be out on the balcony, where he could at least breathe properly and think straight. He took a delicate sip from the glass of vodka in his hand and as he admired the beauty of his own lawns and listened to the noise from the party indoors he reflected on his life and the way it had worked out, so predictable to him.

The pain in the back of his neck came entirely without warning. A swift screeching agony flashed across his mind, abruptly giving way to an unbearable ache in his neck. He could feel his own blood warm in the midnight air dribbling down the back of his tuccido and frothing and gurgling from his mouth. The glass dropped from the lifeless hand and the body slumped over the railings.

Over the noise of the party, nobody heard the glass shatter on the floor below; and nobody heard the tall dark figure withdraw his knife and cautiously vanish across the lawns, not even arousing the guard on the gate as he quietly tumbled over the wall and away.

It was midday the following morning when the ortopsy was to be carried out. Shortly before this time the doctor in charge of the operation made his way down the corridor towards the operating theatre in haste behind, his young assistant trotted to catch up. "You're late" said the elder man his tired, wrinkled face bearing no expression and his cold eyes staring constantly in front. "I know, I'm sorry, I had a late night last night and a rushed morning, you know what

Its' is always wrong.

I mean?" he asked, out of breath "No replied the doctor calmly as they entered the operating theatre.

After a brief inspection of the body the young man murmered "He's in a bad way" the elder doctor was more wizened to this type of operation, but he was inclined to agree.

"So that's the verdict? stabbed with a poisoned blade?" came the voice, low pitched and surprised. It reached the doctor through a haze of cigar smoke, behind which sat a stout man, fairly tall and middle aged. He had little hair on top of his head but a thick moustache resting neatly on his upper lip. To the doctor he resembled a cartoon character tossed from an uncanny slapstick world into the harsh realities and responsibilities of being chief of Police.

"Then the two ARE in common" he muttered, half to himself" sorry sir? What do you mean?"

" I mean the other murder of the victims father in his home a few minutes later" answered the chief. Confusion stormed across the doctor's mind. "Killed by the same knife, same finger-prints and all" he added.

"Thankyou chief" said the puzzled doctor as he left the room. His friend the elder doctor had questioned a witness who had seen a tall, strange looking man heading south towards the city centre, the victims father lived in the Northern suburbs. " There is no way anybody could have covered the distance between the two killings in a car let alone on foot," he thought.

The mysterious murders barely raised an eyebrow for the police, but hard as he tried the

Check carefully the punctuation of dialogue.

young doctor could not get it out of his mind, it ate him up slowly and it raced through his mind and it reflected in the stern looks he gave to everybody. Black lines appeared under his eyes and for nights sleep seemed impossible.

It was quite by accident that he stumbled across a clue to the mystery. The newspaper headlines dictated in large, bold letters seemed trivial to the doctor and it was a small article within the paper that aroused his interest. A convict had been released by accident and was on the loose within the city. A small photograph showed two south American men, they were identical twins and both had a heavy mass of jet black hair and around a very rounded chin one of them had an unshaven face. None of them looked particularly evil, except for the eyes. Both had two eyes seemingly identical. They were dark and paled the rest of the faces.

The headlights proved the only light in the darkened alley except for a flickering lamplight which spluttered light like a dying man. High walls surrounded the street and a gang of black youths eyed the car suspiciously as it casually rolled around the corner. It made down the street at a speed of 5 MPH. The headlights lit up the alley and made the automobile resemble a panther stalking its prey. It smoothly silenced to a halt, next to a surprised old man with a bottle in his hand. The doctor stepped out with a smile, "Hello Nicky" he said. Nicky's face bore an expression of distrust "Hello" he answered suspiciously "I won't beat about the bush. Nicky what I want to know is where can I find these two" he handed the man

Slang – only in dialogue

the newspaper " I don't know" snapped Nicky drinking like a glutton from a flask. The doctor handed him a 5$ note " It's coming" He started " It's coming" the doctor handed him another 5$ note and Nicky confidently gave him an address. It took many hours searching but finally the doctor found the house. He stopped the car with a purr from the engine stepped out and inspected the building, he then decided to take a gun with him, from the glove department he produced a hand pistol. Without knowing it the doctor in his anxiety had left the keys in the car.

The dark, depressing building was near the centre of the city and many similar structures stood looming over it. All the windows were smashed and the door hung on by one hinge. He cautiously stepped over the door and made his way across the cold stone floor. Rusty water dropped from the ceiling with a plonk and filled the room with an eerie atmosphere like a clock ticking away uncannily.

At the far end of the room a door was shut and the doctor, his heart racing approached the door and slowly turned the knob to open it, the face peered over him and he reeled backwards with a scream, it was the eyes, the eyes that scared him as he knelt on the floor trembling, he pulled out the revolver as the man approached slowly. He felt the cold steel of the gun on the back of his head and he froze with a yell and a tear.

Outside Nicky was waltzing past, merry though not drunk, he heard a shot echo and die in the cool midnight air. He spotted the car

Should this have a question mark

looking graceful, but out of place in the slummy street like a panther in a cage. Noticing the keys, he approached it and clammered in. He had not reached the end of the street when for the second time the air was split, this time by a screeching explosion, the street was lit up as the car vicously exploded and burned out fiercly.

Essay Six

The great temple of the city of Atlantis. Imposing and majestic, it rose above the level of the other buildings of the city. It had spires which elevated towards the open sky and the high points echoed the far stars, which were slowly fading away into the sun's wide path. The temple, built of the grey, black-veined soapstone, reflected the slowly moving sunlight and it shimmered with the pale golden glow of the sun.

The sky, dark on the West horizon, was slowly but surely lightening. The Eastern horizon began to minutely pulse with signs of pastel fire and life, streaking lazily across the sky, to herald the coming of the sun again.

The city, quiet in the smallest hours of the morning, was lit from the East and its great, graceful silhouette stretched further to the Greacian suburbs. It tapered towards the Southern Forum and disappeared within metres of the softly waving sea, lapping the shores of the port and its golden band of running sand.

The Northern Guard Tower overlooked the great city, evoking a feeling of security from the tall, slim, stone warrior. It marked the confines of the city to the North, where it changed instantly into open, rambling, green hedges and fields of scarlet poppies and amber grain. These crimson and golden fields were interleaved with large meadows of green, verdant, natural growth with the sustenance for the bovine and

Do the paragraphs follow on naturally?

equine populace of the Island.

The city's people had returned before the morning and would not awake for some hours yet. Meanwhile, the open forums and curved amphitheatres were empty but graceful in the fact of their emptiness. Great walls surrounded each forum and each theatre, containing the music and the speech of the sleeping Atlanteans.

The domes of the many giant habitations were apparent, like so many bubbles resting in the city's solitude, almost ready to float away at the slightest zephyr. The steps to the domes' foundations were like monstrous, elegant ziggurats which snaked up and down to the cliff-like walls of the domed villas.

Lying in their slowly rocking berths were the slim, elegant ships of the innovative Atlanteans. Like lengths of mink fur, they seemed to flow in and out of the water, the waterline shifting slightly now and then to compensate for the movement of the liquid surface of the sea.

The port curved around the natural inlet of the Island and the Atlantean Islers had taken advantage of this and built around it, lining the inlet with great blocks of marble, black, white-veined chunks from the foundations of the city.

The sea, many-hued, flowed like liquid air and gave the port a life, a living green, blue, aqua, turquoise — it flowed in one colour and out of another, sparkling

Cheque the spelling of words witch sound alike.

and shimmered with occasional flecks of pure white foam, blanched under the guidance of the sun and sea.

The sky by now had become a cacophony of pastel clouds which floated in a pale grey-blue expanse of sky. The sea gulls of the ocean bantered and shrieked at the sea thrushes which glowed momentarily and then had flown by with their tiny, powerful wings. This mass of pinions became spread across the liberated morning sky and depopulated the airwaves.

The air above the sky shimmered and thickened into a blanket of brightness. This faded away, settling into the city and then the city woke with the aid of the sun's blanket of warmth. A coruscation of sound arose from the silent-before-city and the sun arose finally to a new day.

The people had woken up but had missed the splendour of the morning. Like a jewel in the crown of the day, the sun shone brightly, close to white light, and the city glowed with this encouragement from the great orb of the sky.

1 hour   Huttson Lo

Plan your writing and give it a structure.

Writing for a practical purpose

Apart from writing to express feelings or opinions, most writing we do is for a practical purpose e.g. to give information, to summarise and report or to get something done. The important things to remember are:

1 **accuracy** and clarity of the language,
2 **language** suited to the purpose and audience,
3 a clear cut **structure**.

Accuracy

Accuracy in particular is important, as there should be no room for misunderstanding or need to interpret. Consider this recipe:

Take some flour, milk and eggs. Mix the flour and milk together and then the eggs for a while until it looks nice. Add some salt and a portion of other seasoning. Bake it in a hot oven until it is done.

Practice

1 List the ways in which the recipe is unsatisfactory and suggest improvements.

2 Computer manuals and do-it-yourself instructions are notoriously confusing. Find examples from them and re-write them so that they can be easily understood.

3 Find examples of ambiguous notices or instructions e.g. 'Tennis shoes only must be worn on the courts'.

Appropriate language

The language should always be formal English (see page 13), even if you are summarising or reporting on informal English.

Should a question mark be inside or outside speech marks?

Structure   The structure should be clear cut and therefore easily seen. Good lay-out, use of headings, appropriate and consistent numbering and lettering, underlining – all these help the reader to see the structure. Study the Information Sheet on page 140 as a good example of information set out in a clear and helpful way.

Good practice guide – summaries

1 Read the passage to be summarised once quickly and a second time more slowly.

2 Study it section by section.

3 Write down the main ideas and the supporting ideas in each section.

4 Leave out lists and examples. Find a general word which sums them all up e.g. instead of 'knives, forks and spoons' say 'cutlery'.

5 Write the notes from number 3 (above) in a continuous form.

6 If you have been asked to summarise only part of the passage make certain you have not included material from the rest.

7 Read over your summary, checking that you have not left out any ideas from the passage.

Good practice guide – reports

1 The layout of the report is important.

2 Use headings and sub-headings.

3 Numbering and lettering of the sections must be consistent.

4 An orderly sequence from section to section.

5 Distinguish between main arguments and supporting arguments.

6 The language must be formal and accurate.

7 Be brief – be clear – be accurate.

Use of headings and sub-headings in reports

Going to the Poly

1 Describe precisely where the following are:
   a the Polytechnic's main library,
   b the railway station,
   c Langham Tower,
   d the Arts Centre.

2 Give precise written instructions for the following:
   a someone driving by car from Newcastle who wants to park the car and visit on foot the Sports Centre, the Police Station and Galen Tower.
   b someone arriving by bus who is going to walk to the main Halls of Residence area calling in at the theatre on the way.

3 Suppose you were a student at the Polytechnic and wanted to persuade a friend to join you there. Write a letter explaining the advantages as far as location and amenities are concerned.

Good description needs good observation

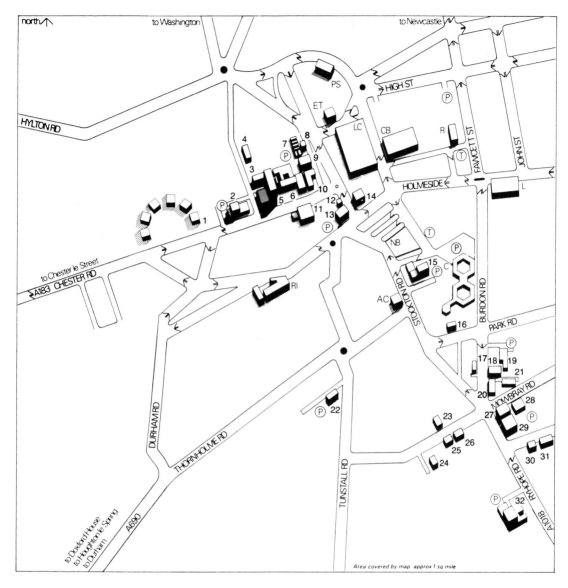

north↗

to Washington

to Newcastle

HIGH ST

HYLTON RD

HOLMESIDE

FAWCETT ST

JOHN ST

to Chester le Street

A183 CHESTER RD

DURHAM RD

THORNHOLME RD

A690

to Doxford House
to Houghton le Spring
to Durham

TUNSTALL RD

STOCKTON RD

BURDON RD

PARK RD

MOWBRAY RD

RYHOPE RD

A1018

Area covered by map approx 1 sq mile

Polytechnic Buildings

1 Polytechnic Precinct
2 Forster Building
3 Sports Centre
4 Life Sciences Building
5 Wearmouth Hall
  Terrapin Huts
6 Edinburgh Building
7 Reprographic Unit
8 Hind Street
9 Hutton Building
10 St. Mary's
11 Main Polytechnic Library
12 Green Terrace
13 Priestman Building
14 Galen Building
15 Benedict Building
16 St. George's House
17 Douro House
18 Clifton Hall
19 Bede Tower
20 Mowbray Villas
21 Westfield Hall
22 Thornhill Park
23 Tasker House
24 Ashbrooke Hall
25 Williamson Hall
26 Park Hall
27 Langham Tower
28 Carlton House
29 Armstrong-James Building
30 Hammerton Hall
31 St. Michael's
32 Backhouse Building

Other Buildings

PS Police Station
LC Leisure Centre
CB Corporation Bus Station
R Railway Station
L Library & Museum
NB National Bus Station
C Civic Centre
RI Royal Infirmary
AC Sunderland Arts Centre
ET Empire Theatre

Other Symbols

⇄ Traffic Flow
Ⓟ Parking facilities
Ⓣ Taxis

Are you repeating yourself?

Healthy eating

The following information is given:

- Table 1: the results of an investigation into school meals.
- A brief analysis of the survey.
- A guide to healthy eating – a fact sheet given out to Surrey schools (see page 140).

Study them closely and then:

1 Write a descriptive report on the eating habits of the students in the survey.

2 Draw up a list of recommendations with examples of balanced menus.

Item	Price	Choice
Hot Selection		
Meat and potato pie	28p	11.3
Beefburger bap	26p	9.2
Pizza	20p	8.0
Hot dog roll	22p	7.2
Beefburger	13p	5.0
Hot dog sausage	10p	4.9
Jumbo sausage	24p	4.2
Cheese and onion flan	21p	3.5
Fish finger	7p	3.5
Cheese pasties	24p	3.1
Chip barm cake	33p	3.1
Chicken and mushroom pie .	30p	3.0
Cottage pie	26p	2.8
Steak and kidney pie	29p	2.3
Beef and onion pie	28p	0.7
Vegetables and Other Accompaniments		
Chips	20p	70.0
Gravy	2p	33.5
Potato cake and butter	11p	14.0
Curry sauce	8p	9.5
Baked beans	10p	5.4
Rice	12p	4.8
Mashed potato	12p	3.0
Mixed vegetables	12p	1.8
Coleslaw	12p	1.3

Item	Price	Choice
Cold Selection		
Plain salad	20p	2.7
Cheese salad	25p	2.5
Cheese salad bap	27p	2.0
Tuna salad bap	35p	2.0
Tuna Salad	35 p	1.2
Corned beef salad	35p	1.0
Sweet Selection		
Chocolate crispies	6p	22.7
Doughnuts	10p	12.3
Flapjack	9p	10.4
Cheesecake	13p	9.2
Chocolate eclairs	13p	8.7
Iced buns	7p	8.5
Yoghurts	16p	7.6
Ice cream	13p	6.7
Lemon buns	13p	6.5
Crumble with custard	13p	4.3
Fresh fruit	13p	4.3
Crumble (no custard)	10p	3.8
Butterfly buns	8p	3.5
Angel whirl	13p	3.2
Jelly and cream	11p	3.0
Scones and butter	13p	1.8
Cream splits	13p	1.4

Table 1. The percentage of 1012 students across all school years choosing different items from the school canteen selection, assuming that they had 60p to spend.

Do not use too many technical terms.

One day's school meals

We then took a look at the kind of foods offered in the school canteen, which is organised on a cafeteria system. We made a note of the menus for one week, and then carried out a survey of the total school population, using a questionnaire based on one day's school menu, which asked them which foods they would choose if they had 60p to spend. We were trying to find out which foods from the menu were most popular with young people. As a result we would then be able to find out the nutritional value of the students' diets, with particular reference to fat intake.

When the 1012 questionnaires had been completed we counted every response for every item on the menu and calculated the percentage choice for each item. The results are shown in Table 1. We then analysed the questionnaires to find the following information:

1. The number of students choosing NO major source of protein.

2. The number of students choosing NO fresh fruit or vegetable other than chips or potato.

3. The number of students choosing BOTH chips and a dessert high in fat and carbohydrate.

Analysis of the school meal survey.
1. 34% of students chose NO major source of protein.

2. 85% of students chose NO fresh fruit or vegetable other than chips or potato.

3. 68% of students chose BOTH chips and a dessert high in fat and carbohydrate.

One of our conclusions from these results was that one-third of our students are choosing meals which contain insufficient protein which is needed for growth. As teenagers are going through a period of growth and development, this was a very worrying finding.

Secondly, a staggering 85% chose NO fresh fruit or vegetable other than chips or potato, and their diets therefore were lacking in fibre and vitamin C.

Thirdly, nearly three-quarters of the students chose both chips and a dessert high in fat and carbohydrate. Therefore, these students had main meals which were made up mainly of fat and carbohydrate, and therefore dangerously low in the more nourishing protein and fruit and vegetable foods.

Recommendations

As a result of our study we would like to put forward the following recommendations:

1. That the school meal menu is quite drastically altered to one which is *more healthy*.

2. The large choice of items on the present school menu should be *reduced*.

3. The school meal menu should contain more *dietary fibre*.

4. Most important of all, there should be a *reduction of the fat and carbohydrate* content of the school menu.

5. A colour coding or 'traffic light' system should be introduced in the school canteen to indicate to students the type of food to avoid.

6. We should aim to *educate* the students in our school into *eating more wisely*, by making them aware of the dangers of the wrong type of diet.

Watch your full stops.

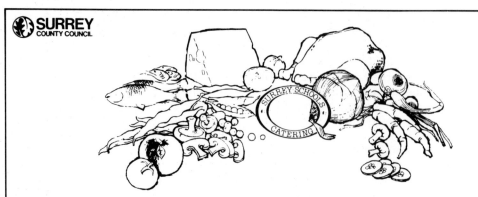

SURREY
COUNTY COUNCIL

PUPILS FACT SHEET: The Traffic Light Guide to Choosing Food for Healthy Living

1. **Why is food choice an important factor in healthy living?**

   The adequacy of our diet perhaps contributes the most to our overall state of health and there is evidence to suggest that a number of illnesses can be directly related to what we eat.

   For example:

   (a) Too much **fat** in the diet can be linked to:
   — heart disease
   — strokes
   — obesity

   (b) Too much **sugar** in the diet can be linked to:
   — diabetes
   — obesity
   — dental decay

   (c) Too much **salt** in the diet can be linked to:
   — high blood pressure

   (d) Too little **fibre** in the diet can be linked to:
   — cancer
   — bowel disorders

2. **What can you do to reduce the risks of these illnesses?**

   Follow these simple recommendations:

   (a) Reduce the amount of
   fat/fatty foods ⎫
   sugar ⎬ in the diet
   salt ⎭

   (b) Increase the amount of fibre in the diet.

   (c) Drink plenty of liquid.

3. **Remember:**

   (a) To watch out for **'hidden sugar'** found in foods like:
   jam
   chocolate
   cakes
   biscuits
   fruit yoghurt
   many puddings

   (b) That as well as butter and margarine, pastry, biscuits, cream and all fried foods are also surprisingly **rich in fat.**

   (c) Try to **avoid adding any salt** to your food – the salt which occurs naturally in our food is sufficient for our needs.

   (d) To **eat more fibre** – include foods such as:
   — bread – especially wholemeal
   — potatoes (without added fat) especially jacket potatoes
   — breakfast cereals – especially those containing bran
   — vegetables, fruits and salads

4. **To help you follow these dietary guidelines –**
   a system of **'traffic light'** food coding has been introduced in school catering.

   Foods high in fat, sugar or salt are coded **RED.**
   Foods high in fibre are coded **GREEN.**
   All other foods are coded **AMBER.**

   When choosing your lunch, aim to

   (a) **Include** plenty of foods from the **green** group.

   (b) **Reduce** the foods selected from the **red** group.

   (c) Choose your lunch mainly from foods from the green and amber groups.

Different tasks require different types of writing.

Casualities

Motorcyclist fatally injured.
Car passenger fatally injured.
Car driver slightly injured.

Conditions

Undulating, 'B' class, country road.
Weather fine.
Road surface damp.
Good daylight conditions.

Causes

Driver lost control of car after mounting a slight, grass verge and crossed the road diagonally before crashing into an approaching motorcyclist. The driver of the car was young, the holder of a provisional licence, but not accompanied by an experienced driver. He had also taken the car without the owner's permission.

Accident

> Practice

1 Describe what happened from the point of view of a spectator. Give the account in a chronological order, that is, in the order in which it happened.

2 Imagine you were the driver of the car and had to make a statement to the police. Write out the statement.

3 Imagine you were the first policeman/woman to reach the scene.
   a Write out your report giving a full account of what you saw when you arrived, the extent of the damage, a summary of the action you took and of the statements from witnesses, and your assessment of the cause of the accident.
   b Make notes that you would use as part of a talk to a group of young people who were on a safety-in-driving course.

Are you writing to the topic?

The young and money

There is no such thing as an 'average teenager' and nothing brings this out more than attitudes to money and saving.

According to detailed opinion surveys on ten to 18-year-olds throughout Britain, parents' attitudes to money are the prime influence on children up to 13. Beyond that, it's an increasingly personal matter.

Moneycare reviews saving and spending trends at school age and beyond.

Under-twelves, whether boys or girls, tend to like to save. Their finances are carefully marshalled, with accumulated cash counted out lovingly at intervals. Saving is as important a concept as spending – saving to save as opposed to saving to spend. 'When I save I feel really chuffed with myself,' says one little girl aged eleven. But, after that, opinion research across the country suggests that saving loses its appeal, and 13 to 15-year-olds spend at least as much as they save.

Once into the real teens and beginning to mature, independence very definitely extends to finances. Spending is dominant among 14 to 16-year-olds, half of whom have some kind of part-time job. Yet that's the time that schoolchildren like to open a bank account of some form. Banks are regarded as 'safe' places to keep money, although the key to a teenager's heart appears to be accessibility.

They all want easy access to their funds with banking hours that fit into their lifestyle, whether still at school or working part-time.

Extra interest rates are not generally of prime importance to these young customers. Teenagers on small allowances or earnings can work out for themselves that an extra half per cent here or there is going to make precious little difference on a bank balance of say £50.

This is the time that school children who do have an interest in opening some form of account – often because their parents suggest it's a way of dealing with cash or cheque gifts from relatives – start to pick up bank leaflets and read them avidly.

They look for a bank which explains its services well, suggesting how they can manage their money and spelling out the facilities available in easy-to-understand language. Oddly enough, boys are more likely to open a bank account than girls at this age – perhaps the Adrian Moles of this world trying to impress their Pandoras. According to the research, boys do want to accept the responsibility of managing money sooner than girls, although that may well be a hangover of parents' attitudes to their roles.

Both sexes tend to despise 'carrots' from banks which are supposed to attract their custom, but which merely remind them too much of their childhood. Any gimmick which smacks of pre-teenage life has a negative effect, although gifts do act as incentives and are carefully weighed up when choosing to open an account. No bank without an incentive pack is seriously considered in the younger grouping. Incentive schemes in themselves bring out a variety of responses among teenagers. To eleven to twelve-year-olds, the incentive pack is something to be prized, treasured and shown around – it is at this age that the appeal is strongest. Fourteen-year-olds show less spontaneous awareness of individual

Where the money comes from

Ages 11–17	£m
Pocket money	466.56
Regular job	1846.99
Errands	250.10
Money from parents for specific purposes	296.04
Occasional money/gifts from relative	262.25
Total for age group	3121.94

Carrick James Market Research National Survey 198

Today's 11 to 17-year-olds get most of their mon from a regular job of some sort. Once into their teens, independence very definitely extends to finances, with most teenagers choosing to spend mainly on clothes, records and snack.

Read over what you have written and correct errors.

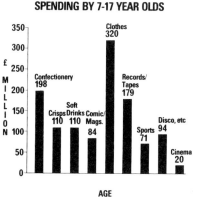

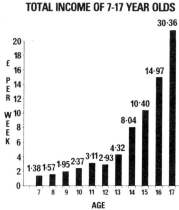

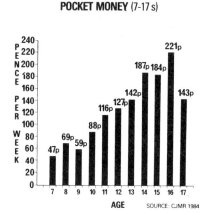

SOURCE: CJMR 1984

schemes, but they enjoy the feeling that they are getting something for nothing.

Girls aged 14 to 16 are more interested in bank facilities and ready access than the actual incentive on offer. And boys of this age see themselves as positively beyond these 'carrots', although they'll salvage a few odd bits from such packs. 'All the gimmicky ones sort of fail,' says one 16-year-old boy.

Older teenagers are really torn between getting their hands on acceptable gifts and being treated as adults whose money is as good as anyone else's.

Bob Larkham, Assistant Marketing Manager at NatWest, explains that 'the young people's market from ten to 18 is acknowledged to be the most difficult market of all – it's all a question of understanding their needs. From the age of 14 upwards, whether our teenagers are at school, at work or furthering their education, we have found they all want ready access to their money.'

Practice

1 The following are taken from the passage. Say whether they are fact or opinion and the reasons why you think this is so.
   a 13 to 15 year olds spend at least as much as they save.
   b Half of 14 to 16 year olds have some kind of part-time job.
   c Extra interest rates are not generally of prime importance to these youngsters.
2 Make notes on the following:
   a the different attitudes towards money of the under twelves and 14 to 16 year olds,
   b the difference between boys' and girls' attitudes to bank services.

3 Study the diagrams and chart and write a report which includes:
   a the amount of money available for spending,
   b where they get the money from,
   c how they spend it.

4 Compare the above (question 3) with your own experience and say how closely it matches it.

Use of headings and sub-headings in reports

Treasure trove

Do you fancy a walk in the country this weekend or even a stroll across the fields in open Green Belt land near your home? You could end up several thousands pounds richer – quite literally.

That happened to a lorry driver near Saffron Walden in Essex, who walked along a stream running through a local estate one Sunday afternoon in March a couple of years ago, and found a hoard of silver and gold coins hidden by a Royalist tax dodger during the Civil War. The British Museum eventually got the coins, but the lorry driver got their full current market value: about £30,000! The wealthy estate owner renounced any claims.

The treasure does not even have to be physically buried in the ground. A year earlier, a Wiltshire trainee catering manager had done very well out of finding a hoard of gold sovereigns and half-sovereigns dating from 1821 to 1859, hidden in the roof of an old country house.

Both sets of coins were 'treasure trove', an ancient legal term dating back over a thousand years. As far back as the early 17th century, Sir Edward Coke, James I's Chief Justice, was writing in his famous 'Institutes': 'Treasure Trove is when any gold or silver, in coin, plate, or bullion hath been of ancient time hidden . . . whereof no person can prove any property, it doth belong to the King.'

Notice that the hoard must have been deliberately hidden. If it was merely lost, abandoned or forgotten, that does not count as treasure trove. How on earth is anyone nowadays to know? A coroner's inquest is convened and all available evidence – about the finding place, the objects found and the views of experts – is considered before the modern decision is given – a sort of exercise in archaeological Agatha Christie.

If the verdict is that the goods were hidden, the coroner rules they are treasure trove – and, as such, the property of The Queen. But you will not lose your financial interest in your find.

The British Museum is given the option of deciding whether it wants to keep them: if it does not, you get the goods back and are free to sell them at the best price you can get. If the Museum keeps them, the Crown – or, to be more accurate, the Treasury – will pay you their current market value. Who assesses that value? Not the British Museum itself – although it used to until 1977. It is thought fairer now for the valuation to be made by a totally independent body, the Treasure Trove Review Committee.

But please, if ever you do find any cache of old coins or ancient treasure of any kind, do not fail to report it to the police, the local coroner or Scottish equivalent, a local museum, or the director of the British Museum. If you don't, you are at risk of being prosecuted for theft (as does happen) for, unless and until a coroner's inquest rules the find is *not* treasure trove, you can be prosecuted for stealing Crown property.

What exactly *is* treasure trove? Does it have to be gold or silver, or does any other kind of precious metal or ancient material qualify?

Almost unbelievably, the question did not arise for decision by the courts until as recently as November 1981. A man with a metal detector – that great new gadget for treasure trove hunters – had arrived at a Lincolnshire farm and asked if he could have access to the fields. He said he was interested in archaeology. The farmer said he could go in – but that nothing was to be removed.

In fact, the searcher found a hoard of 7,800 Roman coins buried in an earthenware urn below ploughshare level. You won't be surprised to learn that he did not tell the farmer, but merely took them away. He sold some. The truth came out. He was prosecuted for theft and given a suspended prison sentence.

The farmer, as is usual with goods found embedded in your land, was given back the coins as his property. But were they treasure trove? A coroner's inquest said they were, but the case went one stage further: to the High Court.

For there was no gold at all, and no more than 18 per cent silver, in the coins. Did that make a vital difference? 'Yes,' ruled Mr Justice Dillon, rejecting a claim brought on behalf of the Crown by the Attorney General of the Duchy of Lancaster.

And he was upheld by the Court of Appeal. Lord Denning, then Master of the Rolls, said that we must follow today what Lord Coke had written over 300 years ago – with the only modern gloss being that the goods must be 'substantially' gold or silver. What did 'substantially' mean? 'It has to be a very considerable amount,' said Lord Denning. 'It should, I think, be 50 per cent or more.' So the farmer got the coins and was free to do what he liked with them.

No one should necessarily be disappointed if some ancient find is *not* ruled to be treasure trove. It can take months for the British Museum to decide what they want to do and for the independent Committee to come up with its valuation.

In March 1976, a nine-year-old boy looking for tadpoles in a North Yorkshire stream came upon a sword embedded in the peatlike bottom of the stream. It turned out to be a 900-year-old silver and iron sword once wielded by an Anglo-Saxon warrior, and beautifully preserved in the mire. It was better than the well-known Fiskerton Sword in the British Museum.

He ran home with it to his parents. They were honest folk and told a local museum promptly of the boy's find. In September 1976, an inquest jury at Richmond, Yorkshire, decided that the sword had been lost or abandoned and was not therefore treasure trove. They accepted the view of an expert that 'perhaps the owner lost it when he had three pints of mead too many, or he might have abandoned it after defeat in battle.'

The result was that the lad sold it at Christie's auction rooms in London seven months later, in April 1977, for some £10,000! It has to be said, in fairness, that the trustees of the landed estate on whose premises the find had been made renounced all their claims as owners of the stream-bed in tribute to the honesty of the boy and his family.

So if you're going hunting for ancient treasure – even if it turns out not to be 'treasure trove' – this weekend, I wish you luck. But remember, as with the Yorkshsire case, honesty really is the best policy. Where at all possible, first obtain the permission of the owner of the land before going on to his property and do not be tempted to keep news of your find from the authorities. It is really rather like going through the Customs when coming back from holiday: the average Customs officer will be so glad to find someone prepared readily to admit that he has got 'something to declare' that he will help him to minimise the amount of duty he has to pay. At least, that has always been my experience.

Practice

1 Set out the information in this passage in note form using headings, paragraphs and numbering as appropriate.
What is Treasure Trove?
What to do if you find treasure.
Who decides whether it is treasure?
Warnings.

2 Pick out the examples given in the passage and say which points they illustrate.

Have you strayed off the subject?

Continuous assessment

You are in control of your own topics and writing

All English courses now have a continuous assessment element in them. This may vary from 20% to 100% of the course. You will have a number of assignments to complete over a period of time and the grades you receive for them will be part of your final examination grade.

Advantages

You can benefit from continuous assessment because:

1 You can take more time over your work.

2 You have the opportunity to revise and correct your work, but not, of course, after it has been graded.

3 The assignments can reflect your own interests rather than topics given by an examiner.

4 You can show a wider range of your writing abilities.

5 The assessment you receive will not depend, as an examination does sometimes, on how well or unwell you feel on a certain day.

6 You are not penalised for being a slow writer.

7 More emphasis is put on how you arrive at a piece of writing (**process**) than merely the piece of writing itself (**product**).

Cautions

However, as with all good things, there are also possible drawbacks. You should keep the following firmly in mind:

8 As you have the opportunity to draft and revise your work, careless mistakes cannot be regarded as tolerantly as they would in an exam with a time limit.

9 Likewise, a narrow range of work will be regarded as a limited outlook and ability.

10 You have to be better organised yourself and keep to a timetable of work. If you fall behind with your assignments you have much more work to catch up on than if you were behind with an essay.

11 If you fail to complete the required number of assignments you could be regarded as being absent from the whole exam.

12 If you are allowed to keep your completed assignments:
   a you must not alter them if they have been graded. To do so could be regarded as cheating and lead to disqualification.
   b you must keep them in a safe place as they will have to be produced towards the end of the course. If you lose them report it straight away.

13 You must not use other people's work, pretending it is your own. If you do so you will be disqualified.

In spite of these possible drawbacks, continuous assessment is a much fairer way of assessing your ability in English and you should take advantage of the benefits it produces.

Language to suit your purpose and audience

Drafting and correcting your work

Ordering and sequencing

You must get into the habit of planning and producing a rough draft, revising it and correcting your work as you go along. For the plan of your work refer to the advice given in 'Varieties of writing' on pages 87 and 88.

Check that

1 in a narrative or account, the incidents are arranged in the most effective way

2 the points of view are well argued

3 that arguments and ideas are developed naturally along with examples

4 that you avoid repeating arguments and ideas

5 that each paragraph follows on naturally from the previous one

6 that there is a structure with a beginning, middle and end. Learn the art of sequencing, i.e. of arranging your material in a way which most effectively achieves the purpose of your writing (see page 85).

Practice

1 Even an obvious sequence may have a different starting point according to the way you look at it, e.g. when does the year begin for the following?

the Western calendar   the Jewish calendar
financial purposes (e.g. taxation)   the Chinese year
a school pupil

Under what circumstances does the same apply to the days of the week?

2 Arrange the following in a better order.
   a Method; 3 lbs of strawberries; 3 lbs of sugar; Leave the jam to cook in a pan until a skin forms; Ingredients: Lemon juice; Put the strawberries, lemon juice and sugar into a pan and heat slowly, stirring it until the sugar dissolves; half an ounce of butter; bring it to the boil and boil it for 10 to 15 minutes; stir it gently and put it into jars and cover them; take the pan off the heat and stir in the butter; How to make Strawberry Jam.
   b Room preparation; pasting; cutting the paper; stripping old paper; measuring up; hanging the paper. How to paper a room; preparation of wall

3 Note the following words which help to establish a sequence.

firstly   initially   at first   first of all
secondly   afterwards   then   next   subsequently
furthermore   in addition   also
eventually   lastly   finally   summing up   in sum

Do the paragraphs follow on naturally?

Choosing the best word

In English there are many words which have roughly the same meaning, but few which mean exactly the same. There is a definite difference between 'a tall woman' and 'a big woman', or between 'a small man' and 'a tiny man'.

The same applies to the opposite, e.g.
What is the opposite of 'live' in the two examples?

a **live** animal
We are now going over **live** to Number 10 Downing Street.

Because of these slight differences in meaning and associations, it is very important that you select the word that suits your purposes best. In particular it is important that you should not confuse words which are similar in meaning or spelling. It is also important to remember that some words have different meanings in different registers (see pages 6–10), e.g.

valve means something different in Engineering, Electricity and Surgery, and **power** has different meanings in Mathematics, History and Physics.

Practice

1 Look at the meaning of the following words and explain the difference between them with appropriate examples.

reluctant	reticent	deceased	diseased
uninterested	disinterested	formally	formerly
effect	affect	principal	principle
advice	advise	stationary	stationery
compliment	complement	review	revue

2 The following are often misused. Consult a dictionary to check the meaning and usage.

alibi   less   fewer   lay   lie   literally   loan

Words state, but also imply.

3 Explain the difference in the meaning and usage between the following groups of similar words and say which are closest to each other.

illness	sickness	disease
obstinate	singleminded	stubborn
advantage	benefit	profit
futile	helpless	useless
plan	project	scheme
meek	mild	patient
anxiety	care	worry
cold	freezing	chilly
easy	simple	uncomplicated
murder	assassinate	execute

4 Certain spelling patterns produce many words which have similarities. Use a dictionary or thesaurus to find words beginning with **squ** and **gl**. Explain what they have in common and in the case of the **gl** words, how there is a slight difference in association.

5 Use a thesaurus to find different words expressing:

speaking, e.g. mumble
walking, e.g. loiter
happiness
theft

Avoid vague words

After a <u>nice</u> long sleep I woke up and as it was a <u>nice</u> day I decided to <u>get</u> up straight away. The water was <u>dead</u> cold in the tank so I <u>got</u> dressed. I had to <u>get</u> my breakfast myself, which was <u>dead</u> mean as my mum and dad had both <u>got</u> jobs which meant that they had to <u>get</u> out early. I really enjoy a <u>nice</u> cup of tea and a <u>nice</u> breakfast but it is <u>dead</u> tight having to <u>get</u> it yourself.

This type of language is quite common in speech but it should be avoided in written English. Even in speech if it is overdone, it can become monotonous and meaningless. There are always other words which give a more precise meaning. It is up to you to find them. Words which should be avoided because they are vague include:

get   awful   awfully   horribly   super   dead (meaning very)
lovely (in some circumstances)   chronic   kind of   things   sort of   loads of
millions of

It is not always possible to avoid words like **get** and **things** but where good alternatives are available they should be used.

Use a dictionary to check spelling.

Unnecessary words

Avoid unnecessary words or redundant expressions, that is expressions which say the same thing twice, as in 'Annual salary of £10,000 per year'.

Practice

1 Include the following expressions in sentences and then rewrite them with the underlined words omitted. Does this change the meaning?

a number of examples
a red coloured dress
few in number
for a period of two days
continued to persist
demanding the imposition of a heavy fine
on the occasion when
new innovations

Ambiguity

Avoid ambiguity, i.e. unintentionally producing two or more different meanings, e.g.

Billy told John that he was late for work.

He in this sentence is ambiguous because it could refer to Billy or to John. Also avoid using a word in its literal sense when you use close by a similar word in a metaphorical sense, e.g.

When it started to rain his face clouded over.

Practice

1 Study the following and explain how they are ambiguous.

Sports Minister wants to stop drinking at football matches.
Health Minister appeals to nurses.
Bring the jam to the boil then sit for 5 minutes on low light.
Elizabeth can do this job as well as Jane.

Sharon told Gillian she was wrong. Who was wrong?

Main errors in grammar

When you are drafting, redrafting and improving what you have written, be on the lookout for errors in grammar. The following are the most common.

Agreement of the subject with the verb

Mistakes in the agreement of the subject with the verb. Plural subjects take plural verbs. **We was**, **you was** are incorrect. It is curious how this is a common mistake yet the equivalent mistake in the present tense is rarely made, e.g. **We is, you is**.

Also, the mistake with **you were** is more common in the question form, e.g. **Was you?**

Problems do arise, however, when the subjects are not obviously single or plural, e.g. collective nouns. **The team is playing away. The team are playing away.** Generally speaking you use the singular if you are thinking of the team as a unit and the plural if you are thinking of them as a collection of individuals. However, this distinction is not always observed. The main point to watch is that you do not change from the singular to the plural or vice-versa, as in:

As the orchestra was playing too slowly, the conductor told them off.

everyone, each, none are strictly speaking singular, e.g.

None of us is perfect

but in spoken English they are often used with a plural verb.

Incorrect form of the past tense of verbs

The different form of past tenses in English often causes problems. In English we can refer to the past by a change in the form of the verb, e.g. **I walked**, **I spoke**, or by using an auxillary verb with another form of the verb itself, which is known as the past participle, e.g. **I have spoken**.

The past participle form **spoken** should not be used as the past tense on its own, **I spoken, I seen it**.

Was we or were we?

Practice

Note and learn the difference between the simple past tense and the past participle in the following verbs.

Present tense	Past tense	Past participle with auxillary verb
I sing	I sang	I have sung
beat	beat	have beaten
break	broke	have broken
do	did	have done
eat	ate	have eaten
fall	fell	have fallen
fly	flew	have flown
hang	hung	have hung
hang (execute)	hanged	have hanged
lay	laid	have iaid
say	said	have said
pay	paid	have paid
lie	lay	have lain
ride	rode	have ridden
write	wrote	have written

Note that the past participle can be used as an adjective, e.g. **written English**, or with the verb 'to be', **The cup was broken**.

Form of pronouns

1 You use the form **I**, **we**, **he**, **she**, **they**, when it is the subject of the verb, i.e. mostly when it carries out the action or is the state of being, e.g.

I could not see where **she** was until **he** came into the room.

For all other circumstances use the form **me**, **us**, **him**, **her** or **them**, that is when it is the object of a verb or governed by a preposition, e.g.

Between **you** and **me**
For **you** and **me**

(Try repeating the word 'for', before me. You would not say 'She did it for you and for I.)

I saw **them** before I recognised **him**.

Strictly speaking **It is I** is correct, but almost everybody says **It's me**.

Between you and I, this is wrong.

2 **Who** is the equivalent of the subject and **whom** is the equivalent form of the object. If a preposition comes directly before **who** you should use the **whom** form, e.g.

The person to **whom** I was speaking paid no attention.

However this is falling out of use, particularly when there is no preposition in front of **who**, e.g.

The person **who** I was speaking to was not paying attention.

3 **Them** should be used instead of a plural noun and not with plural nouns, e.g.

Them boys did it. *should be*
Those boys did it. *or* **They** did it.

Adjectives and Adverbs

The form that causes most errors is the use of the comparative and superlative, see page 95.

Common errors in punctuation

1 The most common error is using a comma when there should be a full stop.

I walked out of the room, I did not like what he said, it was also too hot, I was tired.

Think of the full stop as Halt! or the red light at traffic lights. When you have completed your statement you Halt! and then start a new statement with a capital letter. Therefore, statement completed – halt! – red light – new statement – space and capital letter – green light to go forward.

2 The position of the apostrophe sometimes causes problems.
   a Use it to indicate where a letter has been dropped out, e.g.

   I am > I'm
   He will > he'll
   I will > I'll

   (What will happen if you omit the apostrophe in the last two examples?)
   b Originally to show possession in English you would add **es** to the end of the noun, e.g.

   the girl > the girles = of the girl

   The **e** dropped out and the apostrophe was used to show that it had been omitted, e.g. **girl's**. The rule is quite simple: if the possessing noun does not end in **s** (e.g. girl, men), add **'s**, (e.g. girl's, men's).
   If the possessing noun does end in **s**, just add an apostrophe after **s**, e.g. girl boys'.

Watch your full stops.

3 Use of inverted commas with speech.
To remember the position of " " (speech marks), always think of speech as the words contained inside the bubbles in a cartoon, e.g.

(Where are you going?)   (I am going home.)

"Where are you going?"   "I am going home."

This can be particularly useful if the verb of saying interrupts what is contained within the bubble.

"Why are you dressed like that?" he asked. "Where are you going?"

"I couldn't find my school tie," he said, "<u>so</u> I put this one on."

Errors with capital letters

1 New sentences start with capital letters. If you use a comma where you should use a full stop, then almost certainly you will not use a capital letter, e.g.

'He is going home, he is feeling sick' *should be*
'He is going home. He is feeling sick'.

2 Capital letters should be used for people's names and for the names of places such as towns, cities and countries, e.g.

Barbara Tilly   Colchester   England   Europe

The names of shops, pubs, theatres are included here as places e.g.

After shopping at Marks and Spencer we had a meal in 'The Dog and Partridge' and afterwards went to the Palace Theatre.

Capital letters for words of a book, play, song title.

3 Capital letters are also used for the main words of titles of books, plays, records, etc. Quotation marks are also used with them, e.g.

I went to the theatre last night and saw 'The Merchant of Venice'.

In print, different type is sometimes used instead of the inverted commas. The effect is the same – to separate the title from the rest of the sentence, e.g.

I went to the theatre last night to see *The Merchant of Venice*.

Main errors in spelling

Correct spelling is important. Rightly or wrongly, your general ability in English may be judged on your ability to spell. Certainly, if there are spelling mistakes in formal letters or reports that you write you will be criticised. Good spelling is therefore a social advantage. Most people have some difficulty with spelling but equally so, most people can learn to spell correctly.

Good spelling can be learned and the following guides or rules should be helpful.

Before learning them remember:

- The vowels are: **a, e, i, o, u,** and **y** when pronounced as **'i' or 'ee'**.
- The consonants are the remaining letters of the alphabet.
- A suffix is a group of letters that may be attached to the end of another word, e.g. **-ing**, **-ness**.

1 **ei** or **ie**

When the sound is **ee**, **i** goes before **e**, except after **c**, e.g.

chief   believe   receive   deceit   (Think – **ece**)

Exceptions: seize   weir   weird

2 final **y**

When a word ends in a **consonant + y**, the **y** changes to **i** if a suffix is added, e.g.

try – tries, beauty – beautiful, cry – cried, happy – happily

Exceptions

a The rule does not apply if the suffix begins with **i**, as in **ing**, e.g.

  cry – crying

b *Note*: say – said, pay – paid, day – daily

3 final silent **e**

Drop the final **e** when a suffix beginning with a vowel is added, e.g.

hope – hoping, *but* hopeful, love – lovable

Exceptions

a The **e** is retained after **c** or **g** when the suffix begins with **a** or **o**, e.g.

  notice – noticeable, manage – manageable, courage – courageous

---

– ece – in receive and similar words

How do you think these words would be pronounced if the **e** was dropped?

b Why is the **e** retained in the following?

dye – dyeing, singe – singeing

c *Note*: due – duly, true – truly, whole – wholly

4 doubling the final consonant
This applies to words ending in a **single vowel** + **single consonant**. When a suffix is added the consonant is doubled.

a if the word is only one syllable (a monosyllable), e.g.

run – running, rot – rotten

b if the accent is on the last syllable, e.g.

occur – occurring, prefer – preferring *but* preference, refer – referring *but* reference

Exceptions   This does not apply to words ending in **l**, e.g.

travel – traveller

5 words ending in **ll**
These words *usually* drop one **l** when they are combined with other words, e.g.

full – hopeful, till – until, fill – fulfil, well – welcome, all – always

The rule does not apply if the word is pronounced as if it is two words, e.g.

bulldog   illness   downhill   foretell

6 **able** or **ible**
This is not a rule but a rough guide. If there is another form of the word ending in **ate** or **ation**, then **able** is correct, e.g.

admiration – admirable

If there is another form of the word ending in **ive** or **ition**, then **ible** will be correct, e.g.

audition – audible, responsive – responsible

7 **cede** or **ceed**
The **ee** form goes with the prefixes **suc**, **ex**, **pro**, e.g.

succeed   exceed   proceed (but not procedure)

With other prefixes the general rule is **cede**, e.g.

precede   intercede   recede

Note: supersede – meaning to take the place of.

8 words ending in **our**
Words drop the **u** with suffix **ous**, e.g.

humour – humorous, labour – laborious

Get your spelling write rite right.

Good practice guide – spelling

1 Many people spell certain words incorrectly time and time again and no matter how often they check the correct spelling. Make your own list of these and always keep it for reference.

2 Have a dictionary handy when you are writing so that you can refer to it.

3 There are spelling rules and guidelines that will help you with your spelling provided that you also learn to put them into practice. Many people know the rules but do not practise them.

4 Try to see a pattern in the correct spelling of words which you often mis-spell, e.g. accommodation is often mis-spelt. Remember **cc, mm** and the first four vowels form a sandwich **aooa**. Business – comes from busy but the **y** changes to **i** when **ness** is added.

5 Learn to visualise the shape or pattern of words so that it looks wrong if it is mis-spelt.

6 When you come across new words, particularly longish ones, learn them; cover them up; test yourself and then check your answer. If it is wrong try to find out the cause of the mistake and in which unit it occurs and then use the learn – cover – test – check method again.

7 Take extra care with words which look or sound alike, e.g.

lose	loose
fair	fare
scene	seen
practice	practise
were	where

8 Remember:
Gud spelling is an advantidge and bad spelling shud look odd.

Cheque the spelling of words witch sound alike.

Overall practice

1 The mistakes in the following sentences are underlined. Write the sentences out with them corrected.

It is a matter for you and <u>I</u> to decide.
<u>Its'</u> no use complaining.
When you <u>recieve</u> the invitation ignore it.
<u>Theres</u> never been a murderer like him in <u>all of past history.</u>
<u>Were was</u> you last night__
I did not see <u>him he</u> was behind the car. <u>As</u> you said__

2 Correct the mistakes or faulty expressions in the following.

Flat 2
Birmingham

Yesterday Dec 9th

Dear sir
    I seen youre advert in the local rag and I thought I could do the job as good as any one else so I hope you'll consider me for it. I left collage last month with a good report. Both Mr. Jone's the principle and Mr. Todd, him as what learnt me english each said I would of got a record of acheivment if I'd staid on but I wanted to get a job. Im not affrayd of working hard and you wont regret it if you let me have a go.

Yours respectively

John Raymond

3 I cant think of nothing more perfect than laying in the sun all day without hardly a breeze to cool you of.

4 After the place w'd lived in for fewer than three months our new accommadation was a site for soar eyes and more superior than anything I seen abroad.

5 As soon as the farmer scrapped the soil of the lid he new h'd found a most unique relic of roman times

6 The team was trying there hardest but they could not score. Personally, me in my opinion I would of changed the gaolkeeper because of the fact that his nerve had gone

7 Its' well known that a dogs' tail when it wags it means its happy.

8 'Where was you' the detective asked when the shot was fired' 'Outside' I said in the yard. 'That means there was less than three people in the house unless you'r trying to decieve me. He continued to persist with that type of questioning without once refering to what he'd been told earlier.

9 In spite of the fact that the cup was obviously broke I'd drank out of it before I realised.

Read over what you have written and correct errors.

10 Between you and I I should have got off of the train at the last station but seeing that barefaoted woman without any shoes and socks on the platform she gave me such I shock I forgot.

11 After we read to kill a mocking bird we saw the film with gregory peck but didnt like it.

12 As it was dark I did not see the stationary bus coming towards me at first, so I decided to swerve and knock the pedestran down who was waiting outside the old brown cow. this lead me to the police station were I am now.

13 Dear Sir please excuse darren not in school yesterday but he had to go to the hospital with his stomach he hadent bean for three days and when he did go he couldn't stop going so I took him to the casualty. It was them pills they said the docter had gave him.

Yours

Mrs Webley

14 Study the way an editor has changed the original draft of the news story on page 161. Consider each change made and say what you think has been achieved by it.

Dear Mrs Smith, – Yours sincerely,

Version A

Twenty-eight tremors have been recorded here following yesterday's earthquake which burst a reservoir about 60 miles north-east of Santiago and buried the village of El Cobre in a sea of mud, the Seismological Institute said today.

Officials said 27 bodies had been recovered from El Cobre and another 121 people were missing out of the 400 inhabitants of the village which was hit by a 1,000 yard wide sea of mud and rock. Other reports put the total toll of the earthquake as high as 600.

Version B

⌐ *EL COBRE, a village of 400, was buried in a 1,000-yard sea of mud after an* ⌐
~~Twenty-eight tremors have been recorded here following yesterday's~~ earthquake ~~which~~ burst a reservoir about 60 miles north-east of Santiago ⌐*yesterday*⊙ ~~and buried the village of El Cobre in a sea of mud, the Seismological Institute said today.~~

⌐Officials said 27 bodies had been recovered ~~from El Cobre~~ and another 121 ~~people~~ were missing⊙ ~~out of the 400 inhabitants of the village which was hit by a 1,000 yard wide sea of mud and rock.~~ / Other reports put the total toll of the earthquake as high as 600.

⌐ *The Seismological Institute reported a further 28 tremors yesterday*⊙

Version C

Nearly 150 of the 400 inhabitants of the village of El Cobre, 60 miles north-east of Santiago, are feared dead, buried beneath a sea of mud and rock produced by an earthquake yesterday.

The violent earthquake—28 tremors were recorded yesterday—burst a reservoir and produced a 1,000 yard wide avalanche of mud and rock. Twenty-seven bodies have been recovered and another 121 people are missing.

(Version A typeset for comparison)

Twenty-eight tremors have been recorded here following yesterday's earthquake which burst a reservoir about 60 miles north-east of Santiago and buried the village of El Cobre in a sea of mud, the Seismological Institute said today.

Officials said 27 bodies had been recovered from El Cobre and another 121 people were missing out of the 400 inhabitants of the village which was hit by a 1,000 yard wide sea of mud and rock. Other reports put the total toll of the earthquake as high as 600.

Be clear – be precise – be accurate.

Reviews

A feature of the GCSE is that you have to read full texts and discuss them. This will usually be done as part of the continuous assessment. The purpose of this is not only to encourage you to read at length, but also to allow you practice in giving your opinions in an orderly, logical way. Although your own reaction to the books, plays, films, etc., is most important, the way you express it is of equal importance. You need to show knowledge of the book, play, programme, etc., describe it, state your reaction and make an assessment.

There are four general steps in any considered criticism.

1 What is the author trying to do? – **writer's purpose**

2 How does he or she try to achieve this? – **the means**

3 How successful is it? – **a critical evaluation**

4 Is the final product worthwhile and what does it mean to you? – **personal reaction**.

The writer's purpose

Never criticise a book for being something it does not intend to be. For example, it would be foolish to criticise a geography textbook for not being exciting or humorous. You can certainly criticise it according to how well or badly it performs as a textbook, i.e. how well it gives information and teaches you on the topic. In this first stage of criticism, therefore, always judge a book on its own terms. You can later, in the fourth stage, give your opinion as to whether those terms are worthwhile in themselves.

The means chosen

What method has the author chosen to put over his ideas? A novel? A short story? Play? Poem? Then within his chosen type of writing, what other means does he use? These are discussed in greater detail below.

Critical evaluation

This should be based on consideration of the first two. What an author intends to do may be quite clear, but what he achieves may be something quite different.

One paragraph – one main topic

Personal reaction   All form of criticism is eventually a personal reaction, but it needs to be based on knowledge, understanding and full consideration of the book. An author's purpose may be quite clear and the means he uses to achieve it may be equally clear and he may be successful in carrying out his purpose, but the final product might not, in your opinion, be worthwhile. This is where your personal opinion, (subjective assessment) should merge with a critical approach (objective assessment).

The following are suggested approaches to writing a review or criticism of novels, plays, films, TV programmes and records. The questions are meant to direct your attention towards important aspects. You should not merely string the answers together as this will not produce a readable criticism. Furthermore the questions are not necessarily in a connected sequence. You should, however, use your answers as the basis of your review.

Novels or stories

The main elements in a novel or short story are **plot** or story line, **characters**, and **background**. In addition you need to consider the **dialogue** and the **language** used by the writer.

Plot or story Line

1 Most stories have a basic pattern. There is the situation at the start, and then difficulties arise causing complications. There is generally a conflict either between people or groups or even ideas and there is generally a sorting out of the complications at the end i.e. **climax** and **denouement**. (Check the meanings of the words 'climax' and 'denouement'.)

2 What type of incidents are in the book? Are they exciting, humorous, romantic or possibly a mystery?

3 The pace of the story is important. In adventure stories the incidents follow on in quick succession. In mysteries the incidents are designed to keep you in suspense. In stories in which the main interest lies in the characters, the pace is more leisurely.

4 Is the story told in the first person (I) or third person (He, she)? Both have advantages and disadvantages.

5 What is the climax to the plot? Do you feel that the problems have been solved and the people reconciled? If you do not, that is not necessarily an adverse criticism. However, most people expect a satisfactory conclusion to a mystery story. Sometimes writers cheat by making the complications so difficult that there is no apparent way out and then they introduce somebody or something out of the blue in order to solve the problem.

Are you behind with your assignments?

Characters

1 Give a brief description of the main characters and the part they play in the development of the story.

2 What is the connection between the main characters and the incidents? Do the characters develop as a result of their experience?

3 How are the characters portrayed, e.g. by the author's description, by what they say, by what they do, by what other characters in the story say about them?

4 How convincing and realistic are they? Does the author let you know not only what they look like but also how their minds work, giving you an insight into their personality?

5 Are you meant to sympathise with or dislike any of them?

6 A stereotype is a type of person that you frequently find in a certain kind of story, e.g. the all-knowing detective, the smooth-talking villain, the gossiping old woman. Are the characters in the story you are reviewing stereotypes or does the author make them into individuals?

Background

1 The background is of importance in many types of novels, e.g. historical fiction, science-fiction, stories concerning country life or life in a city. It may be of importance in thrillers or mysteries but not necessarily so.

2 How well is the background described? How realistic is it?

3 Is there a balance between description, actions and dialogue? Many people do not like books that have too much description in them.

Dialogue

1 Is the dialogue appropriate to the speaker?

2 Does it help to portray the character?

3 Does it help to carry the story line along?

Check carefully the punctuation of dialogue.

Language

1 Is the novel easy to read? In some novels the writing is very compact and dense which makes for slow reading.

2 Is the vocabulary used easy to understand and can you follow the sentence structure and paragraphs?

Plays

Many of the considerations that apply to novels regarding plot and characters also apply to plays. However we need to consider the following as well:

1 Visual appeal, that is the setting, costumes and special effects.

2 In a novel the author tells the story; in a play the plot or story unfolds before your eyes on the stage.

3 The acting is therefore of great importance. Are the actors audible? Are the gestures overdone or exaggerated? This may be deliberate as in some comedies or farces.

Films or TV plays

Again, many of the elements are the same as for a play or novel, but it is the camera which tells the story, shows the characters in action and portrays the setting more convincingly than a stage set can. If you are writing a review of a film or TV play, you need, therefore, to consider the cinematic techniques of:
- close-ups,
- panoramic views,
- cutting from one scene to another (if this is done frequently and suddenly it can be confusing),
- fading,
- superimposing sound or vision on a scene,
- background music.

Note that in a film the dialogue does not have to be as full as in a play or novel. There are many long sequences without any dialogue whatsoever.

Reviewing a record

1 Give the details, i.e. single or album; artists, main and backing; cost and possibly a brief description of the cover.

2 Give the reader some idea of the type of music; comparison with similar or previous disc by the singer can be helpful.

3 Are the lyrics important?

4 Assess the performance of the artists.

5 Give your overall impression and judgement.

Don't use a comma where you should have a full stop.

Practice

1 On page 168 is a review of a non-fiction book. Read it carefully and assess how good it is. If you feel it is lacking in any way, suggest improvements.

2 On pages 169 to 173 there is a short story by L. P. Hartley. Write a review of it along the lines suggested on pages 162–165. Remember that in a short story the writer does not have time to develop the characters or to introduce many incidents. The story has to make its impact in a few pages.

3 Write reviews of two contrasting records in this week's charts.

4 What do you think a good review of a video game should tell you?

5 Write a review of the video of a pop song.

6 Write reviews of the folowing TV programmes:
   a a comedy series
   b a soap opera
   c a police/gangster series

7 Describe the stereotypes of character, action, background, and dialogue you will find in the following:
   a Western   d Who-dunnit?
   b Cops and Robbers film   e Horror film
   c Carry On film

8 Compare the presentation of the news on BBC and ITV.

9 Compare a book you have read with the way it has been presented as a film or on TV.

10 Compare a British soap opera with an American one.

Good practice guide – reviews

In the following, the words 'book' and 'writer' can refer equally to a play, record, film, TV, radio programme.

1 Give factual information about the topic of the review.

2 Show knowledge of the topic – describe – assess.

3 Do not criticise a book, etc. for not being something it does not set out to be.

4 Writer's purpose – means of achieving it – critical assessment – your reaction.

5 Your review should have an order and structure.

6 In a review of a novel/story, the summary of the plot should not be more than one-third of the review.

Is there a structure in your writing?

Book review – Ben, the story of Ben Hardwick

by Esther Rantzen and Shaun Woodward

This is a very moving book about two year old Ben Hardwick and his mother's fight to give him life. The story is told simply and clearly bringing tears to ones eyes when reading it. It contains two sets of lovely pictures of Ben and it has letters from viewers who had written into That's Life. The story itself, is told through diaries kept at the time.

Ben was born with the liver disease, biliary atresia. By the time he was 1 months he had had two kasai operations to save him but they both had failed. His parents, Debbie and Billy, were told that he would only live to two years of age. When Debbie contacted That's Life Ben had just celebrated his second birthday. The only thing which would save Ben would be a liver transplant. However, there was a great lack of donors. This was because doctors were too upset to ask the bereaved parents of potential donors if their child's organs can be used for transplantation. However, Debbie thinks that it would be comfort to the parents if they knew that their child had saved another's life. This point is strongly repeated through the letters from parents whose child has died saying that it would be a comfort to them if their child's organs had been used. They wished that they had had a chance to save anothers life.

Although Ben was originally going to be sent to America for his transplant a liver became available in England so Ben had his transplant here. He recovered very quickly indeed. The donor child was two year old Matthew Fewkes. It was only because the doctor had seen That's Life that he was able to ask Mr. & Mrs. Fewkes if Matthew's liver could be used. T.V. films of Ben's recovery were shown and the nation was captured by him. His sweet appealing face, his bright eyes and his cheery happy smile entranced everyone as well as the courage and determination of his mother.

Tragically Ben only lived for one more year – a second transplant failed. This year was priceless to all who knew and loved him. His parents had a normal healthy child for a short time. In a short, significant life he revolutionised transplant surgery and his example saved hundreds of lives. A few of these children's stories are told in the book. One boy was 11 year old Matthew Whittaker. His parents were told that he would live to two. He became a medicle miracle. He had his transplant (only because of Ben though) and is alive today.

It is a simple, well written book telling all the details of Ben's life and expressing the need for donors. It tells of the courage of Ben, Debbie and Billy, Julie and Darryl Fewkes, the Whittakers and all the unheard donors. Without donors this book couldn't have been written.

The proceeds of the book go to the BEN HARDWICK MEMORIAL FUND. This is a trust set up to help to give financial support to successful treatment centres for saving children's lives.

An excellent book – well worth reading. £3.25.

Incorrect speling should luck odd.

The Waits

Christmas Eve had been for all the Marriners, except Mr. Marriner, a most exhausting day. The head of the house usually got off lightly at the festive season, lightly that is as far as personal effort went. Financially, no; Mr. Marriner knew that financially quite a heavy drain was being made on his resources. And later in the evening when he got out his cheque-book to give his customary presents to his family, his relations and the staff, the drain would be heavier. But he could afford it, he could afford it better this Christmas than at any other Christmas in the history of his steadily increasing fortune. And he didn't have to think, he didn't have to choose; he only had to consult a list and add one or two names, and cross off one or two. There was quite a big item to cross off, quite a big item, though it didn't figure on the list or on the counterfoil of his cheque-book. If he saw fit he would add the sum so saved to his children's cheques. Jeremy and Anne would then think him even more generous than he was, and if his wife made any comment, which she wouldn't, being a tactful woman, he would laugh and call it a Capital Distribution – 'capital in every sense, my dear!'

But this could wait till after dinner.

So of the quartet who sat down to the meal, he was the only one who hadn't spent a laborious day. His wife and Anne had both worked hard decorating the house and making arrangements for the party on Boxing Day. They hadn't spent the time in getting presents, they hadn't had to. Anne, who was two years older than Jeremy, inherited her mother's gift for present-giving and had made her selections weeks ago; she had a sixth sense for knowing what people wanted. But Jeremy had left it all to the last moment. His method was the reverse of Anne's and much less successful; he thought of the present first and the recipient afterwards. Who would this little box do for? Who would this other little box do for? Who should be the fortunate possessor of this third little box? In present-giving his mind followed a one-way track; and this year it was little boxes. They were expensive and undiscriminating presents and he was secretly ashamed of them. Now it was too late to do anything more: but when he thought of the three or four friends who would remain un-boxed his conscience smote him.

Silent and self-reproachful, he was the first to hear the singing outside the window.

'Listen, there's some carol-singers!' His voice, which was breaking, plunged and croaked.

The others all stopped talking and smiles spread over their faces.

'Quite good, aren't they?'

'The first we've had this year,' said Mrs. Marriner.

'Well, not the first, my dear; they started coming days ago, but I sent them away and said that waits must wait till Christmas Eve.'

'How many of them are there?'

'Two, I think,' said Jeremy.

'A man and a woman?'

Jeremy got up and drew the curtain. Pierced only by a single distant street-lamp, the darkness in the garden pressed against the window-pane.

'I can't quite see,' he said, coming back. 'But I think it's a man and a boy.'

Its' is always wrong.

'A man and a boy?' said Mr. Marriner. 'That's rather unusual.'

'Perhaps they're choristers, Daddy. They do sing awfully well.'

At that moment the front-door bell rang. To preserve the character of the house, which was an old one, they had retained the original brass bell-pull. When it was pulled the whole house seemed to shudder audibly, with a strangely searching sound, as if its heart-strings had been plucked, while the bell itself gave out a high yell that split into a paroxysm of jangling. The Marriners were used to this phenomenon, and smiled when it made strangers jump: to-night it made them jump themselves. They listened for the sound of footsteps crossing the stone flags of the hall, but there was none.

'Mrs. Parfitt doesn't come till washing-up time,' said Mrs. Marriner. 'Who'll go and give them something?'

'I will,' Anne said, jumping up. 'What shall I give them, Daddy?'

'Oh, give them a bob,' said Mr. Marriner, producing the coin from his pocket. However complicated the sum required he always had it.

Anne set off with the light step and glowing face of an eager benefactor; she came back after a minute or two at a much slower pace and looking puzzled and rather frightened. She didn't sit down but stood over her place with her hands on the chair-back.

'He said it wasn't enough,' she said.

'Wasn't enough?' her father repeated. 'Did he really say that?'

Anne nodded.

'Well, I like his cheek,' Even to his family Mr. Marriner's moods were unforeseeable; by some chance the man's impudence had touched a sympathetic chord in him. 'Go back and say that if they sing another carol they shall have another bob.'

But Anne didn't move.

'If you don't mind, Daddy, I'd rather not.'

They all three raised questioning faces to hers.

'You'd rather not? Why?'

'I didn't like his manner.'

'Whose, the man's?'

'Yes. The boy – you were right, Jeremy, it is a boy, quite a small boy – didn't say anything.'

'What was wrong with the man's manner?' Mr. Marriner, still genial, asked

'Oh, I don't know!' Anne began to breathe quickly and her fingers tightened on the chair-back. 'And it wasn't only his manner.'

'Henry, I shouldn't –' began Mrs. Marriner warningly, when suddenly Jeremy jumped up. He saw the chance to redeem himself in his own eyes from his ineffectiveness over the Christmas shopping – from the general ineffectiveness that he was conscious of whenever he compared himself with Anne.

'Here's the shilling,' Anne said, holding it out. 'He wouldn't take it.'

'This will make it two,' their father said, suiting the action to the word. 'But only if they sing again, mind you.'

While Jeremy was away, they all fell silent, Anne still trying to compose her features, Mr. Marriner tapping on the table, his wife studying her rings. At last she said:

Plan your writing and give it a structure.

'They're all so class-conscious nowadays.'

'It wasn't that,' said Anne.

'What was it?'

Before she had time to answer – if she would have answered – the door opened and Jeremy came in, flushed and excited but also triumphant, with the triumph he had won over himself. He didn't go to his place but stood away from the table looking at his father.

'He wouldn't take it,' he said. 'He said it wasn't enough. He said you would know why.'

'I should know why?' Mr. Marriner's frown was an effort to remember something. 'What sort of man is he, Jeremy?'

'Tall and thin, with a pulled-in face.'

'And the boy?'

'He looked about seven. He was crying.'

'Is it anyone you know, Henry?' asked his wife.

'I was trying to think. Yes, no, well, yes, I might have known him.' Mr. Marriner's agitation was now visible to them all, and even more felt than seen. 'What did you say, Jeremy?'

Jeremy's breast swelled.

'I told him to go away.'

'And has he gone?'

As though in answer the bell pealed again.

'I'll go this time,' said Mrs. Marriner. 'Perhaps I can do something for the child.'

And she was gone before her husband's outstretched arm could stop her.

Again the trio sat in silence, the children less concerned with themselves than with the gleam that kept coming and going in their father's eyes like a dipping headlight.

Mrs. Marriner came back much more self-possessed than either of her children had.

'I don't think he means any harm,' she said, 'he's a little cracked, that's all. We'd better humour him. He said he wanted to see you, Henry, but I told him you were out. He said that what we offered wasn't enough and that he wanted what you gave him last year, whatever that means. So I suggest we give him something that isn't money. Perhaps you could spare him one of your boxes, Jeremy. A Christmas box is quite a good idea.'

'He won't take it,' said Anne, before Jeremy could speak.

'Why not?'

'Because he can't,' said Anne.

'Can't? What do you mean?' Anne shook her head. Her mother didn't press her.

'Well, you are a funny girl,' she said. 'Anyhow, we can but try. Oh, and he said they'd sing us one more carol.'

They set themselves to listen, and in a moment the strains of 'God rest you merry, gentlemen' began.

*

Good description needs good observation

Jeremy got up from the table.

'I don't believe they're singing the words right,' he said. He went to the window and opened it, letting in a puff of icy air.

'Oh, do shut it!'

'Just a moment. I want to make sure.'

They all listened, and this is what they heard:

'God blast the master of this house,
Likewise the mistress too,
And all the little children
That round the table go.'

Jeremy shut the window. 'Did you hear?' he croaked.

'I thought I did,' said Mrs. Marriner. 'But it might have been "bless", the words sound so much alike. Henry, dear, don't look so serious.'

The door-bell rang for the third time. Before the jangling died down, Mr Marriner rose shakily.

'No, no, Henry,' said his wife. 'Don't go, it'll only encourage them. Besides I said you were out.' He looked at her doubtfully, and the bell rang again louder than before. 'They'll soon get tired of it,' she said, 'if no one comes Henry, I beg you not to go.' And when he still stared at her with groping eyes she added:

'You can't remember how much you gave him last year?' Her husband made an impatient gesture with his hand.

'But if you go take one of Jeremy's boxes.'

'It isn't a box they want,' he said, 'it's a bullet.'

He went to the sideboard and brought out a pistol. It was an old-fashioned saloon pistol, a relic from the days when Henry's father, in common with others of his generation, had practised pistol-shooting, and it had lain at the back of a drawer in the sideboard longer than any of them could remember

'No, Henry, no! You mustn't get excited! And think of the child!'

She was on her feet now; they all were.

'Stay where you are!' he snarled.

'Anne! Jeremy! Tell him not to! Try to stop him.' But his children could no in a moment shake off the obedience of a lifetime, and helplessly they watche him go.

'But it isn't any good, it isn't any good!' Anne kept repeating.

'What isn't any good, darling?'

'The pistol. You see, I've seen through him!'

'How do you mean, seen through him? Do you mean he's an imposter?'

'No, no. I've really seen through him,' Anne's voice sank to a whisper. saw the street lamp shining through a hole in his head.'

'Darling, darling!'

'Yes, and the boy, too –'

'Will you be quiet, Anne?' cried Jeremy from behind the window curtai 'Will you be quiet? They're saying something. Now Daddy's pointing the gu at him – he's got him covered! His finger's on the trigger, he's going to shoo

---

With dialogue, vary the verbs of saying.

No, he isn't. The man's come nearer – he's come right up to Daddy! Now he's showing him something, something on his forehead – oh, if I had a torch – and Daddy's dropped it, he's dropped the gun!'

As he spoke they heard the clatter; it was like the sound that gives confirmation to a wireless commentator's words. Jeremy's voice broke out again:

'He's going off with them – he's going off with them! They're leading him away!'

Before she or any of them could reach the door, Mrs. Marriner had fainted.

The police didn't take long to come. On the grass near the garden gate they found the body. There were signs of a struggle – a slither, like a skid-mark, on the gravel, heel-marks dug deep into the turf. Later it was learnt that Mr. Marriner had died of coronary thrombosis. Of his assailants not a trace was found. But the motive couldn't have been robbery, for all the money he had had in his pockets, and all the notes out of his wallet (a large sum), were scattered around him, as if he had made a last attempt to buy his captors off, but couldn't give them enough.

L. P. Hartley

Different tasks require different types of writing.

Topic work – assignments

This part of the syllabus allows you to write about your own interests, explore your own culture and develop your own ideas. It is particularly suitable for multi-cultural or ethnic minority activities which possibly may not be fully reflected in other parts of the syllabus. It is also an opportunity to link your English work with your studies in other subjects. This cross-curricular approach is one which the GCSE encourages.

As it is part of your coursework, you must pay particular attention to planning, drafting and correcting your work (see pages 148–158). The following are topics which have produced good interesting work from students. In the first group, there are also indications of the wide variety possible for each topic. They are meant to be only suggestions and guidelines. You will probably find many of your own ways of tackling the subject, but you should show knowledge of it, describe and assess it.

The royal family

their history
the royal family and the Press
the cost of the monarchy
influence on fashion
fund raising and charities

the royal family and politics
character studies of individuals
ambassadors abroad
an anthology of writings about them
reading list and bibliography

Old age

statistics
problems the old have with finance
health
independence
family's duties
Government's duties
organisations which help the elderly
describe three or four contrasting people
interview some about what life was like when they were young and their
   opinion of modern life
old age as portrayed in novels, poems and paintings

Do not repeat 'then' too often.

Leisure   leisure and work and unemployment
growth in leisure facilities and organisations
description of a theme park, safari park, seaside funfair
influence of micro-electronics
division of leisure between the sexes
attitude of different age groups
leisure as an occupation
political parties and leisure
is leisure a social problem?
education for leisure
effect of leisure on family life

Are you repeating yourself?

Teenage magazines

survey of the variety and costs
analysis of the types of articles
image of girls portrayed in them
image of boys portrayed in them

advertising in them
the stories in them
what purpose they serve
how they could be improved

Smoking

the history
why people start smoking
statistics of sales and tax
smoking and health

smoking and advertising
as a social problem
how to give it up

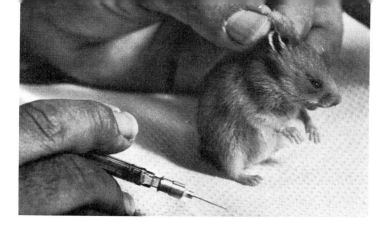

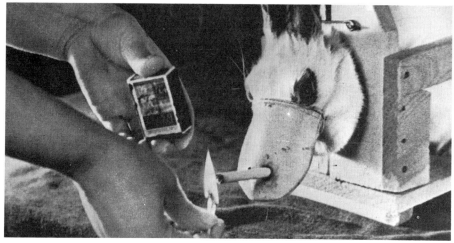

Our attitude to animals

as pets
for food – vegetarianism
cruelty to animals
zoos and safari parks, circuses
preservation of endangered species

use of animals in research
hunting animals for sport
animals and the fur trade
intensive farming methods
animal rights organisations

The British press

its history
the range of newspapers available
the daily papers
local papers
Sunday papers
the free press
statistics – sales – prices

an analysis of two or three
  contrasting papers
advertising in the papers
presentation of news
use of photography
the press and politics

Are you writing to the topic?

Other topics

Pop music
The people and legends/music of . . . (e.g. Ireland, Jamaica)
Marriage in other cultures, e.g. Hindu, Moslem, Jewish
Comparison between a British family and a foreign one
Handicapped people
Teenage fashion
Soap operas
Advice on the twenty records/cassettes you would suggest to someone starting
    a music collection
A planned reading list for 11–14 year olds.
A programme of reading and TV which you would advise for a foreigner
    wanting to get to know and understand the British way of life
Stars of TV or film
Hair styles
Nuclear energy
Information technology in our lives

Good practice guide – assignments

1 Decide which aspects of the topic you are going to deal with.

2 Collect information and material.

3 Select the relevant material and look for variety.

4 Arrange it in a structured order.

5 Make a detailed plan.

6 Do a rough draft.

7 Check the structure of the draft by summarising each paragraph into one short
   phrase.

8 Write out the good copy paying attention to:
   vocabulary
   sentence structure
   punctuation
   spelling

Can you distinguish between fact and opinion?

Spoken English

Stand up! Speak up! Listen with care!

Introduction

Spoken English is the English you are going to use most frequently. You will use it to communicate needs, instructions, advice, ideas and emotions. It is the way in which most people will communicate with you.

To be able to express yourself clearly and effectively is to possess a valuable skill. It is also important to be a good listener. Speaking and listening skills can be developed and improved by good planning, preparation and practice.

Some general points

A sense of audience

What sort of audience are you going to speak to? Is it a group of your fellow students? If so you will probably be in tune with their interests and their level of understanding. Is it a large group or a small intimate group which will allow you to try a more personal and intimate style?

If you are preparing a talk for very young children, the material and vocabulary will have to be within their range of understanding. The age, experience, knowledge and interests of the audience are all factors to take into consideration.

▲ What do you think they are listening to? Is the reaction of the adults different to that of the children?

Dialect and slang

Dialects, patois and slang are all forms of the language and may sometimes be considered as languages in themselves. These forms of the language are part of people's culture and are important in preserving a sense of identity. They are used to communicate with people who understand and share the dialect or patois, and are therefore of limited use when communicating with those outside the group.

Once again, you must be aware of your audience. It is important to develop skills in the use of English which can be understood by as wide a range of people as possible.

Aids to confidence

You are standing in front of an audience. All eyes are on you. Your mouth feels dry. Is it a bad dream? No. You are about to give a talk to the class. What can you do to help overcome nerves and shyness?

Thorough preparation is the most important thing. If you really know what you are going to do, most of the anxiety should be removed. A set of cards with the headings and very brief notes of each point of your talk can be helpful. As you finish with a card you can put it down or move it to the back of the set.

Useful visual aids can be a confidence booster. You can direct the attention of the audience towards something other than yourself from time to time and this does give you a feeling of control.

Some speakers find it difficult to look the audience directly in the eyes. Do try to look in the direction of the audience. This is much better than looking down at your notes all the time. A desk or table in front of you can also help to give you a sense of security.

Who is your audience?

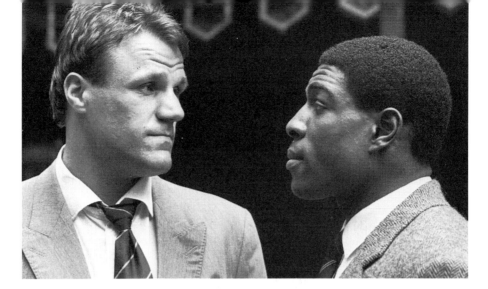

Clarity of speech

Take care to sound your words properly. Regional accent is not important but dropping **h** from the beginning of words, and **t** and **g** from endings will affect the clarity of your speech. You are aiming for clear and effective communication.

Pause and emphasis

Many students have a tendency to rush when talking or reading in front of an audience. Try to control your pace to suit the material or passage. Pauses can be very effective in the right places. Emphasise important words or phrases to draw the audience's attention to them.

Mannerisms

Most of us have habits of speech or movement which are sometimes exaggerated when we are nervous. We may say 'er' or 'um' too often, pull at an ear lobe or scratch our heads. These mannerisms can spoil the flow and the clarity of our speech or distract the audience from what we are saying. Try to identify any such mannerisms and control them.

Ask your fellow students, your teacher what your mannerisms are. Watch yourself in a mirror when practising. Listen to yourself on tape.

Are you speaking too quickly?

Individual work

Giving a talk

Choosing a topic Choose a subject you are well acquainted with or are interested in. Do not go to the nearest encyclopedia and search for an exotic subject, make a few notes and then expect to be able to give a talk on it. You will probably be stumped if there are questions from the audience.

We all have some knowledge or experience we can talk about. Often we do not believe that others will find it interesting. This is a problem of confidence.

You can talk about a hobby or sport you enjoy, a place you have visited, an interesting person, a topic from another subject you are studying, a matter of social concern or a subject of topical interest.

Choose an area you can deal with in the time you have at your disposal. For example, a talk about how to be a good mid-field player is more easily dealt with in five minutes than a talk entitled, 'Football'. A talk on 'The Ear' is a more realistic topic than 'The Human Body'.

The following is a selection of topics on which students have given interesting talks under examination conditions:

The Battle of Agincourt	Pole-Fishing
The Human Digestive System	The Titanic
Looking after a Tortoise	Batting and Bowling Techniques
A Recent Holiday	Making a Sponge Cake
Smoking is Bad for Your Health	The Great Houdini
James Dean	A Visit to Wembley
The Bronte Family	A Hydro-electric Power Station
Venice	Food Additives
Interpreting Dreams	Mardi Gras
Palmistry	Chinese New Year Celebrations
Radio Controlled Models	Gary Sobers
The Moto-Cross Bike	Ramadhan

Good speech is more than words.

Preparation   Your talk must have a plan or structure. A brief introduction can include your reason for choosing the subject. You should then develop your talk in a logical ordered way moving as naturally as possible from one section to the next. Try not to finish too abruptly but round off with a brief conclusion before asking for questions.

Decide which areas of your topic you are going to cover and then decide on the best order. Below is an example of a topic with some possible aspects or sections:

After deciding which areas you are going to cover you can then put them in order, e.g.

Archery
1 Introduction
2 Brief historical background
3 Bows – ancient and modern
4 Other equipment
5 Techniques
6 Competitions and scoring
7 Personal experiences.

The next step is to prepare more detailed notes. A separate card for each section is a good idea.

Visual aids can help to clarify points and can help your confidence but be sure that they are relevant. Visual aids for a talk on 'Archery' could be:

1 Diagrams of Persian laminated bow and English long-bow – on blackboard.

2 Bracer and tab (arm and finger guard)

3 Coloured diagram of target

4 Modern competition bow – or diagram.

The final set of notes for this topic could look like the notes on page 186.

Check your visual aids before starting.

1 Introduction

A little known sport but one which has much to offer

---

2 Evidence of ancient civilizations using bow for hunting and warfare.

---

3 Persian etc. laminated bows
 * Use visual aid of laminated bow
 - explain layers and curves.

---

4 * English long bow
 * Visual aid - diagram on board.
 Yew trees.
 Agincourt and wet bow strings

---

5 Modern competition bow
 * Show bow - or diagram and Arrows
 - explain parts.
 Demonstrate stringing

---

6 Other equipment
 * Show and explain. Bracer
 Tab
 Demonstrate technique of drawing the bow with explanation

---

7 Competitions and scoring

 * Coloured diagram of target

---

8 Personal experiences
 When and why I took up the sport
 Personal progress
 Where you can join a club.

* Indicates visual aid
 to be used

Delivery

Wait until your audience are ready to listen. Stand quietly until you have their attention.

Look up as much as possible so that the audience feel that you are talking to them. Try to include all parts of the audience and remember to speak clearly so that those people at the back can hear.

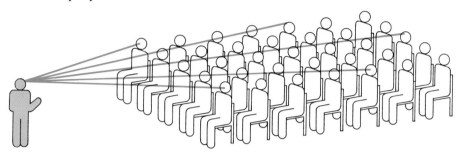

If you are speaking to an audience seated in rows, try to glance at each section in turn as indicated in the diagram above.

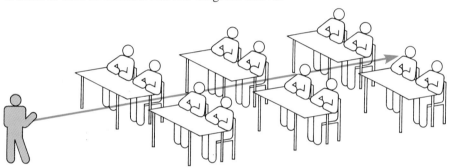

Where there is an arrangement like this you may achieve a closer rapport with the audience by moving up the aisle between the rows as you give your talk. You may also let them have a closer look at the visual aid in this way.

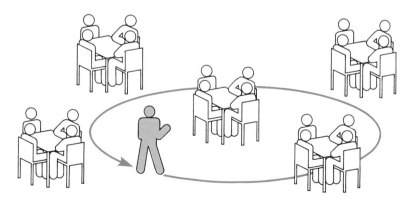

You may have to address people who are seated round small tables and you can achieve a good contact with the audience if you move among them, rather like a cabaret singer.

Don't look at the floor.

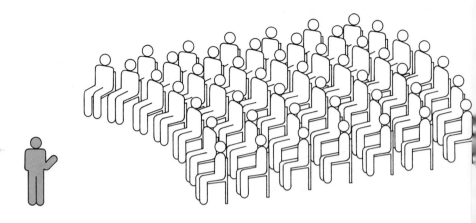

If you have the opportunity, you should arrange the audience to suit you. Rather than have to address people spread over a large room, arrange the chairs in a semi-circle near to you.

Dealing with questions

Question time should be seen as an opportunity for you to expand on your talk. Sometimes a simple question may allow you to develop a point you have only touched on.

Be confident in your treatment of silly questions or ones about obscure points of fact. The honest answer is the best one. 'I don't know but I can find out', is often a fair reply.

A check list

Make yourself a simple check list.

Date and time of talk	
Notes completed	
Talk rehearsed and timed	
Visual aids prepared and marked on notes	
Chalk, bluetac and other equipment	
Seating arrangements checked	

Speak up, don't mumble, speak clearly.

Teachers' notes Check the:

1 availability of room,
2 seating arrangements,
3 equipment required: blackboard, overhead projector, screen, chalk.

Good practice guide – giving a talk

Do:

1 prepare brief notes
2 note where to use your visual aids
3 wait for silence
4 look at the audience
5 speak clearly
6 give the audience time to see your visual aids when you use them
7 indicate when you have finished and ask for questions

Do not:

1 write out the talk fully
2 pass things round while you are talking
3 read to the audience
4 speak with your back to the audience
5 mumble
6 use slang and ungrammatical expressions
7 use visual aids which cannot be seen easily by all the audience

---

How many um's and er's to the minute?

Prepared readings

Choosing a passage

You should choose a passage which will interest and entertain your audience and which will allow you to demonstrate as wide a range of reading skills as possible. Look for something which will enable you to convey mood, emotions, tension or humour. Conversation will give you the chance to show variety of tone and expression.

Preparation

Read the passage through more than once to get familiar with it. Make a note of any words which you are not sure how to pronounce or which you do not know the meaning of.

Practise reading aloud in front of a mirror and look up as often as possible. Listening to yourself on tape can be useful. Mark places in the passage where pauses are required.

Introduction to the passage

Your passage may be interesting in itself but you should introduce it so that the audience can appreciate it more fully. Introductions should be brief but informative and should give the background to the passage and any necessary information about relationships between the characters.

Avoid a monotonous tone or delivery.

Delivery

Do not begin until the audience is quiet. Speak clearly so that all of the audience can hear. Sound beginnings and endings of words. Resist the temptation to hurry – unless it is really appropriate. This is a common fault. Make effective use of pauses. Remember to aim for suitable variety of tone and expression. Try to bring out character and mood.

Vary your pace to suit the content. If there is violent action in the passage, you will often find that the sentences are short and you should quicken your pace. Look up as often as possible – an occasional glance helps to make your audience feel that you are interested in reading to them. Take notice of indications in the passage, e.g. 'I whispered', 'I demanded'.

Questions

You may be required to answer questions after your reading. The most common questions are, 'Why did you choose that passage', or 'What happens at the end of the book?' You may wish to say that the passage gives some of the flavour of the book or is amusing or may tempt people to read the book.

You may not have read the complete book from which the passage is taken. Do not be afraid to admit to this. You could be questioned about your responses to the situation described in the passage or your feelings about the characters.

Avoid one word answers. Try to use questions as an opening to demonstrate your oral skills.

Good practice guide – a prepared reading

Do:
1 prepare thoroughly
2 check pronunciations and meanings
3 wait for silence
4 introduce the passage properly
5 remember pauses
6 speak clearly and expressively
7 look up as much as possible

Do not:
1 chance reading something you have not prepared
2 rush through it
3 mumble
4 read anything you do not understand
5 answer 'Yes' or 'No' to questions

Alter the pitch and volume of your voice.

| Practice |

Before reading the two passages, take note of indications of tone and emphasis, e.g.

Passage 1: 'said Mr. Pumblechook conceitedly'   (line 34)
             'said Mr. Pumblechook testily'   (line 66)

Passage 2: 'I whispered'   (line 1)
             'I demanded'   (line 5)
             'my father bellowed in disgust'   (lines 26–27)

The punctuation in the passage should indicate questions and pauses, but in the following two examples additional indications are given to help with expression.

Key
/   = pause
//   = longer pause
____ = stress

Passage 1 – Great Expectations

Help with expression

When Uncle Pumblechook speaks to Pip he is bullying. He pretends to know more than he does in fact know. He speaks in a worldly-wise, know-it-all manner when he talks to Pip's sister.

Pip's sister is aggressive and ill-natured in her dealings with Pip, but ingratiating and deferential when speaking to Uncle Pumblechook. She looks up to him because he is a successful tradesman.

As Pip's lies became more and more outrageous, his sister cannot hide her amazement. Uncle Pumblechook is also impressed but he does his best to cover his feelings. Pip begins humbly but gets stubborn. When he starts to lie he becomes bolder and more abandoned.

Suggested introduction

This is a passage from Great Expectations *by Charles Dickens. Pip, a young boy who lives with his sister and her husband the blacksmith, has been sent to play at the big house in the village at the request of the mysterious Miss Havisham. When he returns home he is cross-questioned by his short-tempered sister and the pompous overbearing Uncle Pumblechook.*

'<u>Well</u>, boy,' Uncle Pumblechook began, as soon as he was seated in the chair of honour by the fire./ 'How did you get on up town?'

I answered, 'Pretty well, sir', and my sister shook her fist at me.

'Pretty well?' Mr. Pumblechook repeated. '<u>Pretty well</u> is no answer. Tell us
5 what you mean by <u>pretty well</u>, boy?'

Whitewash on the forehead hardens the brain into a stage of obstinacy perhaps. Anyhow, with whitewash from the wall on my forehead, my obstinacy was adamantine. I reflected for some time, and then answered as if I had discovered a new idea,/'I mean pretty well.'

10 My sister with an exclamation of impatience was going to <u>fly</u> at me – I had no shadow of defence, for Joe was busy in the forge – when Mr. Pumblechook interposed with '<u>No! Don't</u> lose your temper. <u>Leave</u> this lad to <u>me,</u> ma'am; <u>leave</u> this lad to <u>me.</u>' Mr. Pumblechook then turned me towards him, as if he were going to cut my hair, and said:

15 '<u>First</u> (to get our thought in order): Forty-three pence?'

I calculated the consequences of replying 'Four Hundred Pound,' and finding them against me, went as near the answer as I could – which was somewhere about eightpence off. Mr. Pumblechook then put me through my pence-table from 'twelve pence make one shilling,' up to 'forty pence make three and four-
20 pence,' and then triumphantly demanded, as if he had done for me, '<u>Now! How much</u> is <u>forty-three pence?</u>' To which I replied, after a long interval of reflection,/'I don't know.' And I was so <u>aggravated</u> that I almost doubt if I <u>did</u> know.

Mr. Pumblechook worked his head like a screw to <u>screw</u> it out of me, and said, 'Is forty-three pence <u>seven</u> and <u>six-pence three fardens</u>, for instance?'

25 '<u>Yes</u>!' said I. And although my sister <u>instantly</u> boxed my ears, it was <u>highly</u> gratifying to <u>me</u> to see that the answer spoilt his joke, and brought him to a dead stop.

'<u>Boy</u>! What <u>like</u> is Miss Havisham?' Mr. Pumblechook began again when he

Distracting mannerisms distract your audience.

had recovered; folding his arms tight on his chest and applying the screw.

30 'Very tall and dark,' I told him.

'<u>Is</u> she, uncle?' asked my sister.

Mr. Pumblechook winked assent; from which I at once inferred that he had <u>never seen</u> Miss Havisham, for she was <u>nothing</u> of the kind.

'<u>Good</u>!' said Mr. Pumblechook, conceitedly. '(<u>This</u> is the way to have him!

35 We are beginning to <u>hold our own</u>, I think, Mum?)'

'I am <u>sure</u>, uncle,' returned Mrs Joe, 'I wish <u>you</u> had him <u>always: you</u> know <u>so</u> well how to <u>deal</u> with him.'

'<u>Now</u> boy! What was she a <u>doing</u> of, when you went in to-day?' asked Mr. Pumblechook.

40 'She was sitting.' I answered, 'in a black velvet coach.'//

Mr. Pumblechook and Mrs Joe <u>stared</u> at one another – as they well might – and both repeated, 'In a black velvet <u>coach?</u>'

'Yes,' said I. 'And Miss Estella – that's her niece, I think – handed her in cake and wine at the coach-window, on a gold plate. And we all had cake and

45 wine on gold plates. And I got up behind the coach to eat mine, because she told me to.'

Was anybody <u>else</u> there?' asked Mr. Pumblechook.

'Four dogs,' said I.

'Large or small?'

50 '<u>Immense</u>,' said I, 'And they fought for veal-cutlets out of a silver basket.'

Mr. Pumblechook and Mrs. Joe stared at one another again, in utter amazement. I was perfectly <u>frantic</u> – a reckless witness under the torture – and would have told them <u>anything</u>.

'Where <u>was</u> this coach, in the name of gracious?' asked my sister.

55 'In Miss Havisham's room.' They stared again. 'But there weren't any horse to it.' I added this saving clause, in the moment of rejecting four richly caparisoned coursers, which I had had wild thoughts of harnessing.

'Can this be <u>possible</u>, uncle?' asked Mrs. Joe. 'What <u>can</u> the boy <u>mean</u>?'

'I'll <u>tell</u> you, Mum,' said Mr. Pumblechook. '<u>My</u> opinion is, it's a sedan

60 chair. She's <u>flighty</u>, you know – <u>very flighty</u> – quite flighty enough to pass he days in a sedan-chair.'

'Did <u>you</u> ever <u>see</u> her in it, uncle?' asked Mrs. Joe.

'How <u>could</u> I,' he returned, forced to the admission, 'when I <u>never</u> see he in my life? Never clapped <u>eyes</u> upon her!'

65 '<u>Goodness</u>, uncle! And yet you <u>have</u> spoken to her?'

'Why, don't you <u>know</u>,' said Mr. Pumblechook, testily, 'that when I hav been there, I have been took up to the outside of her door, and the door ha stood ajar, and she has spoken to me <u>that</u> way. Don't say you don't know <u>that</u> Mum. However, the boy went there to <u>play</u>. What did you <u>play</u> at, boy?'

70 'We played with flags,' I said. (I beg to observe that I think of myself wit amazement, when I recall the lies I told on this occasion.)

'Flags!' echoed my sister.

'Yes,' said I. 'Estella waved a blue flag, and I waved a red one, and Mis Havisham waved one sprinkled all over with little gold stars, out at the coach

75 window. And then we all waved our swords and hurrahed.'

Can those at the back hear you?

'Swords!' repeated my sister. 'Where did you get swords from?'

'Out of a cupboard,' said I. 'And I saw pistols in it – and jam – and pills. And there was no daylight in the room, but it was all lighted up with candles.'

'That's true, Mum,' said Mr. Pumblechook, with a grave nod. 'That's the
80 state of the case, for that much I've seen myself.' And then they both stared at me, and I, with an obtrusive show of artlessness on my countenance, stared at them, and plaited the right leg of my trousers with my right hand.

Passage 2 – Black Boy

Suggested introduction

This is a passage from Black Boy *by Richard Wright. The book is about a black childhood in the southern United States. After Richard's father has complained because a kitten has disturbed his daytime sleep, Richard, who hates his father, hangs the kitten to spite him.*

'I killed'im,' I whispered.

'You did bad,' my brother said.

'Now Papa can sleep,' I said, deeply satisfied.

'He didn't mean for you to kill'im,' my brother said.

5 'Then why did he tell me to do it?' I demanded./

My brother could not answer; he stared fearfully at the dangling kitten.

'That kitten's going to get you,' he warned me.

'That kitten can't even breathe now,' I said.

'I'm going to tell,' my brother said, running into the house./

10 I waited, resolving to defend myself with my father's rash words, anticipating my enjoyment in repeating them to him even though I knew that he had spoken them in anger. My mother hurried toward me, drying her hands upon her apron. She stopped and paled when she saw the kitten suspended from the rope.

15 'What in God's name have you done?' she asked.

'The kitten was making noise and Papa said to kill it,' I explained.

'You little fool!' she said. 'Your father's going to beat you for this!'

'But he told me to kill it,' I said.

'You shut your mouth!'

20 She grabbed my hand and dragged me to my father's bedside and told him what I had done.

'You know better than that!' my father stormed.

'You told me to kill 'im,' I said.

'I told you to drive him away,' he said.

25 'You told me to kill 'im,' I countered positively.

'You get out of my eyes before I smack you down!' my father bellowed in disgust, then turned over in bed./

Who is your audience?

I had had my first triumph over my father. I had made him believe that had taken his words literally. He could not punish me now without risking hi
30 authority. I was happy because I had at <u>last</u> found a way to throw my criticism of him into his <u>face</u>. I had made him feel that, if he whipped me for killing the kitten, I would <u>never</u> give serious weight to his words again. I had made him know that I felt he was cruel and I had done it without his punishing me

But my mother, being more imaginative, retaliated with an assault upon my
35 sensibilities that crushed me with the moral horror involved in taking a life All that afternoon she directed toward me calculated words that spawned in my mind a horde of invisible demons bent upon exacting vengeance for wha I had done. As evening drew near, anxiety filled me and I was afraid to go into an empty room alone.

40 'You owe a debt you can <u>never</u> pay,' my mother said.

'I'm sorry,' I mumbled.

'Being <u>sorry</u> can't make that kitten *live* again," she said.

Then, just before I was to go to bed, she uttered a paralysing injunction she ordered me to go out into the dark, dig a grave, and bury the kitten.

45 'No!' I screamed, feeling that if I went out of doors some evil spirit would whisk me away.

'Get out <u>there</u> and <u>bury</u> that <u>poor kitten,</u>' she ordered.

'I'm scared!'

'And wasn't that <u>kitten</u> scared when you put that <u>rope</u> around its neck?' she
50 asked.

'But it was only a kitten,' I explained.

'But it was <u>alive,</u>' she said. 'Can you make it live again?'

'But Papa said to <u>kill</u> it,' I said, trying to shift the moral blame upon my father.

55 My mother whacked me across my mouth with the flat palm of her hand.

'You stop that <u>lying!</u> You knew what he meant!'

'I didn't!' I bawled.

She shoved a tiny spade into my hands.

'Go out there and dig a hole and bury that kitten!'/

60 I stumbled out into the black night, sobbing, my legs wobbly from fear Though I knew that I had killed the kitten, my mother's words had made i live again in my mind. What would that kitten do to me when I touched it Would it claw at my eyes? As I groped toward the dead kitten, my mothe lingered behind me, unseen in the dark, her disembodied voice egging me on

65 'Mama, come and stand by me,' I begged.

'<u>You</u> didn't stand by that <u>kitten,</u> so why should <u>I</u> stand by <u>you?</u>' she asked tauntingly from the menacing darkness.

'I can't touch it,' I whimpered, feeling that the kitten was staring at me with reproachful eyes.

70 'Untie it!' she ordered.

Shuddering, I fumbled at the rope and the kitten dropped to the pavemen with a thud that echoed in my mind for many days and nights. Then, obeying my mother's floating voice, I hunted for a spot of earth, dug a shallow hole and buried the stiff kitten; as I handled its cold body my skin prickled. When

---

Match your language to your purpose and audience.

75 I had completed the burial, I sighed and started back to the flat, but my mother caught hold of my hand and led me again to the kitten's grave.

'Shut your eyes and repeat after me,' she said.

I closed my eyes tightly, my hand clinging to hers.

'Dear God, our Father, forgive me, for I knew not what I was doing . . .'

80 'Dear God, our Father, forgive me, for I knew not what I was doing,' I repeated.

'And spare my poor life, even though I did not spare the life of the kitten . . .'

'And spare my poor life, even though I did not spare the life of the kitten,' 85 I repeated.

'And while I sleep tonight, do not snatch the breath of life from me . . .'/

I opened my mouth but no words came. My mind was frozen with horror. I pictured myself gasping for breath and dying in my sleep. I broke away from my mother and ran into the night, crying, shaking with dread.

90 'No,' I sobbed.

My mother called to me many times, but I would not go to her.

'Well, I suppose you've learned your lesson,' she said at last.

Contrite, I went to bed, hoping that I would never see another kitten.

What is the purpose of your talk?

Other types of individual work

Reports

A **report** should be concise and informative. You can make brief notes using the card system as you would for a talk. Good organisation is important – have your points in a clear order and sum up briefly at the end.

The person who has chaired a debate or group discussion can give a report on the proceedings outlining:

1 the main arguments presented by the speakers,

2 the quality of the contributions from the audience,

3 the response from the audience,

4 the result of any vote.

A report could be given of a film concert, visit or book. This type of report could be in the form of a review and include your personal response. Reporting on a film, for example, you could consider: story and themes, acting, photography, direction (see pages 162–165).

Explanation or instruction

Explain a specific process or piece of work to a group of people, or give instructions, for example, explain:

The Carburettor
The Human Heart
The Formation of U-Shaped Valleys
How to Drive a Car
How to Cross London by the Underground System
How to Change a Baby's Nappy
How to Use a Launderette

Try to give these explanations without visual aids. You will need to be well-organised and clear.

Written English and spoken English are different.

Narrative and anecdote

Tell a short story to a group of people. This can be an account of an incident from your own experience or one that you have heard. The technique used for prepared readings should be used. Vary your tone and pace to suit the material and attempt to convey character, emotion and mood. Uses pauses to good effect.

Consider the response you wish to get from your audience and work towards it. Do you want to make them laugh or cry, be thoughtful or angry?

Group work

Discussions

The size of the group

The size of the group can be anything from two upwards. The numbers involved will have an effect on the contribution made by the individual members. The smaller the group, the more opportunities there will be for each person to speak, but sometimes if the group is too small, there may be a lack of variety of input. Two people discussing a topic on which they hold the same views may find it difficult to sustain a good discussion.

Seating arrangements are important. Members of the group should sit reasonably close to each other and should be able to see each other. If there is an audience, this should not dominate the seating arrangements.

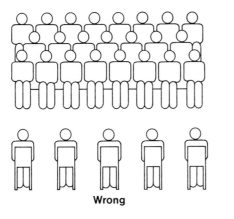

Wrong

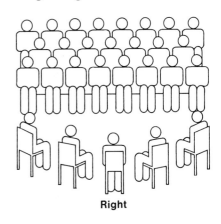

Right

Is the room arranged for your best advantage?

Chairperson

The person in the chair should be impartial and fair but should not be a mere referee. A good chairperson can draw speakers into the discussion, encourage them to explain their points and avoid undue domination of the group by one speaker.

Watch a good chairperson in action, for example, Sir Robin Day on BBC 1 *Question Time* or listen to *Any Questions* on the radio and you will find that the chairing makes an important contribution to the discussion.

Draw a speaker into the discussion by asking him or her what their response is to the last statement. Encourage speakers to enlarge or explain their replies.

Choice of topic

All members of the group should be able to join in the discussion. Remember this when choosing a topic. Try to choose a subject which will interest members of the group. A topic of immediate interest is often a good starting place. For example, a group could discuss arrangements for a Christmas, or end of term party at school or college, including refreshments, decorations, music, date of party and price of tickets.

This kind of discussion has an end product, in this case, the arrangements for the party. The chairperson will wish to reach agreement on these matters.

Look at your audience.

Teachers' notes This type of discussion should produce a report back from one of the members of the group, summing up the discussion and the decisions made, to be assessed as a piece of individual work.

Practice

Look at a selection of the day's newspapers. After you have spent some time looking at them, discuss the news of the day with the aim of choosing items to be included in a five minute news bulletin.

The chairperson should aim to get agreement on the items to be included, their order of priority and the time to be allocated to each.

Other types of discussion may be more open ended. Political, religious and moral discussions often end without fundamental changes in the views held by members of the group.

Suggested topics

Arrangements for taking a group of small children to the seaside
A decorating scheme for the Common Room
Arranging an open day at your school or college
US missiles in Britain
Positive discrimination

Continuous assessment or exams?
How to reduce football hooliganism
Facilities for youth in your area
How should teachers be assessed?
Is alcohol a bigger menace than other drugs?

Preparation A discussion without preparation can be a disaster. You should have time to consider the topic and to make some notes of points or areas of discussion you are going to talk about.

The notes should be limited to a brief list of reminders. You are not preparing a talk or speech. For example: In a group discussing arrangements for taking small children to the seaside, a member of the group might note the following points to discuss:

Number of children
Dividing them into groups
Group leaders
Times of departure and arrival, etc.

Food and drink
First Aid Box
Activities when at the seaside

'Y'know' and 'sort of like' – how many to the minute?

Discussion A discussion is an exchange of views, not a series of speeches. Listen to what is being said and take it into account in your replies. A person who listens and asks questions can make more contribution than someone who tries to dominate.

Try to judge when an area of the topic has been sufficiently dealt with and suggest the next stage to examine. If a member of the group is being left out, try to involve them by asking their opinion.

Points to note
1 Judge the success of the discussion – whether you are a member of the audience or a member of the group.
2 Did the discussion have an end product? e.g. to organise an event?
3 Was the end achieved?
4 Was there a good exchange of views?
5 Was there progress?
6 When assessing individuals, consider:
   a clarity of speech,
   b sentence structure and vocabulary,
   c ability to listen and respond to the views of others,
   d ability to develop arguments clearly and logically.

Good practice guide – group discussion

Do:	Do not:
1 prepare and make notes	1 dominate the discussion
2 listen to others	2 make a lengthy speech
3 ask questions	3 be repetitive
4 bring others into the discussion	4 interrupt rudely
5 use factual information and personal experience	5 use ridicule or sarcasm

---

Teachers' notes TV current affairs programmes and discussions of newspaper reports are good starting points for discussions – especially if the students take notes. Where there is little difference of opinion it may be presented as an interesting exercise for one of the students to take an opposing viewpoint to stimulate the discussion.

Listen to the other person before answering.

Group readings

The size of the group

The group can consist of two or more people, but it should not be so big that members are unable to make a significant contribution.

You should respond to each other within the group. Seating arrangements are important.

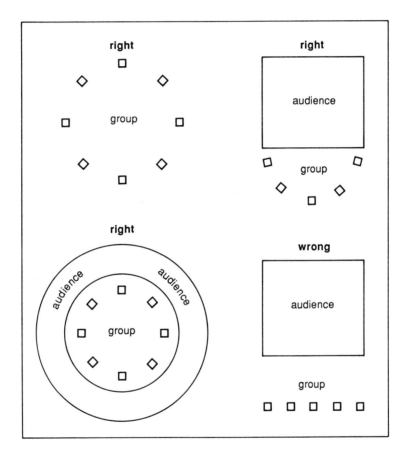

Choice of passage Choose a passage which will allow members of the group to show their skills and which has a reasonable balance of content for each reader. Usually it is best if each member reads one part as doubling-up often causes confusion and weakens the effect of the reading.

You may choose a passage from a novel. One of the members reads the narrative and the others read the words spoken by the characters. With practice, this can be a very effective form of reading.

Discuss the choice of passage within the group.

1 Why this passage?

2 Is it exciting, moving or funny?

3 Is it a suitably self-contained episode to be interesting?

4 Does it offer reasonable scope for members of the group to show their reading skills?

5 How long will it last?

Teachers' notes Students reading very small parts need not be assessed in the same way as the others. However, such contributions may be taken into consideration in long-term assessments.

Preparation 1 Make sure you understand the whole passage.

2 Are there any unfamiliar words?

3 Find out what they mean and how to pronounce them.

4 Practise your own part but, more importantly, practise as a group.

5 Discuss character, tone of voice, pauses and emphasis. Help each other by making suggestions and by positive criticism.

Prepare your talk or reading.

Teachers' notes   The students' contributions to the process of preparation can be assessed as well as their performance in the final reading.

Introduction   A brief introduction will help your audience to understand the piece and to enjoy it fully. Give some background to the situation and to the characters.

An alternative is for each member of the group to introduce the character he or she is reading.

Delivery
1 Speak clearly so that every member of the audience can hear.
2 Sound the beginnings and endings of words.
3 Vary the pitch and tone of your voice suitably.
4 Consider the pace of your reading. If the character is excited, the pace often quickens. When weary or sad, the pace will slow down.
5 Pauses can be very effective.
6 Do not be afraid of silences.
7 Listen to the others and respond to their readings.

Check list

Read the whole passage	
Difficult or strange words?	
Rehearse your part	
Discuss	
Read together	
Organise introduction	
Seating arrangements	

Can those at the back hear you?

Practice

Here are some passages which are suitable for group readings with suggested introductions.

Passage 1 – Julius Caesar

It is just after three in the morning. Brutus, a prominent Roman has been discussing with several fellow conspirators, a plot to murder Caesar. After they have gone, Portia, his wife, enters. She senses he is troubled but does not know of the murder plot.

Enter PORTIA

PORTIA: Brutus my lord.

BRUTUS: Portia! What mean you? Wherefore rise you now?
   It is not for your health thus to commit
   Your weak condition to the raw cold morning.
PORTIA: Nor for yours neither. Y'have ungently, Brutus,
   Stole from my bed: and yesternight at supper
   You suddenly arose, and walked about,
   Musing and sighing, with your arms across;
   And when I asked you what the matter was,
   You stared upon me with ungentle looks.
   I urged you further; then you scratched your head,
   And too impatiently stamped with your foot.
   Yet I insisted, yet you answered not,
   But with an angry wafture of your hand
   Gave sign for me to leave you. So I did,
   Fearing to strengthen that impatience
   Which seemed too much enkindled, and withal
   Hoping it was but an effect of humour,
   Which sometime hath his hour with every man.
   It will not let you eat, nor talk, nor sleep;
   And could it work so much upon your shape,
   As it hath much prevailed on your condition,
   I should not know you Brutus. Dear my lord,
   Make me acquainted with your cause of grief.
BRUTUS: I am not well in health, and that is all.
PORTIA: Brutus is wise, and were he not in health,
   He would embrace the means to come by it.
BRUTUS: Why so I do. Good Portia go to bed.
PORTIA: Is Brutus sick, and is it physical
   To walk unbraced and suck up the humours
   Of the dank morning? What, is Brutus sick?
   And will he steal out of his wholesome bed,

Are you speaking too quickly?

To dare the vile contagion of the night,
And tempt the rheumy and unpurged air,
To add unto his sickness? No my Brutus,
You have some sick offence within your mind,
Which, by the right and virtue of my place,
I ought to know of: and upon my knees,
I charm you, by my once commended beauty,
By all your vows of love, and that great vow
Which did incorporate and make us one,
That you unfold to me, your self, your half,
Why you are heavy, and what men tonight
Have had resort to you; for here have been
Some six or seven, who did hide their faces
Even from darkness.

BRUTUS: Kneel not, gentle Portia.

PORTIA: I should not need, if you were gentle Brutus.
Within the bond of marriage, tell me Brutus,
Is it excepted I should know no secrets
That appertain to you? Am I your self
But as it were in sort or limitation,
To keep with you at meals, comfort your bed,
And talk to you sometimes? Dwell I but in the suburbs
Of your good pleasure? If it be no more,
Portia is Brutus' harlot, not his wife.

BRUTUS: You are my true and honourable wife,
As dear to me as are the ruddy drops
That visit my sad heart.

PORTIA: If this were true, then should I know this secret.
I grant I am a woman; but withal
A woman that Lord Brutus took to wife.
I grant I am a woman; but withal
A woman well-reputed, Cato's daughter.
Think you I am no stronger than my sex,
Being so fathered, and so husbanded?
Tell me your counsels, I will not disclose 'em.
I have made strong proof of my constancy,
Giving myself a voluntary wound
Here in the thigh. Can I bear that with patience,
And not my husband's secrets?

BRUTUS: O ye gods,
Render me worthy of this noble wife!   [*Knocking within*]
Hark, hark, one knocks. Portia go in awhile,
And by and by thy bosom shall partake
The secrets of my heart.
All my engagements I will construe to thee,
All the charactery of my sad brows.
Leave me with haste.

Alter the pitch and volume of your voice.

Passage 2 – Liverpool Miss

This passage is from the second part of Helen Forrester's autobiography.
Helen's parents are middle-class but have come down in the world. The family
live in very poor circumstances but Helen's mother wants her to stay at home to
look after the house. After secretly applying for a job in a sweet shop, she is
asked to go for an interview. There is a family row but eventually Helen is
allowed to go accompanied by her mother.

It was a very little shop, in a shabby block of other small shops and offices. Its
window, however, sparkled with polishing despite the overcast day. Through
the gleaming glass I could dimly see rows of large bottles of sweets and in front
of them an arrangement of chocolate boxes, all of them free of dust. Beneath
the window, a sign in faded gold lettering advertised Fry's Chocolate.

Mother, who had not spoken to me during the walk, paused in front of the
shop and frowned. Then she swung open the glass-paned door and stalked in.
I followed her, my heart going pit-a-pat, in unison with the click of Fiona's
shoes on the highly polished, though worn, linoleum within.

An old-fashioned bell hung on a spring attached to the door was still tinkling
softly when a stout, middle-aged woman with a beaming smile on her round
face emerged through a lace-draped door leading to an inner room.

'Yes, luv?' she inquired cheerfully.

'I understand that you wrote to my daughter about a post in your shop?'
Mother's voice was perfectly civil, but the word 'post' instead of 'job' sounded
sarcastic.

The smile was swept from the woman's face. She looked us both up and
down uncertainly, while I agonised over what Mother might say next.

'Helen?' the woman asked, running a stubby finger along her lower lip.

'Helen Forrester,' replied Mother icily.

'Ah did.' The voice had all the inflections of a born Liverpudlian. She looked
past Mother, at me standing forlornly behind her. Her thoughtful expression
cleared, and she smiled slightly at me. I smiled shyly back.

I felt her kindness like an aura round her and sensed that I would enjoy
being with her, even if she did expect a lot of work from me.

'Have you ever worked before, luv?' she asked me, running fingers on which
a wedding ring gleamed through hair which was improbably golden.

I nodded negatively. Then cleared my throat and said, 'Only at home.'

'What work would Helen be expected to do?' asked Mother, her clear voice
cutting between the woman and me like a yacht in a fast wind. She had also
the grace of a yacht in the wind; but the sweet-shop owner was obviously
finding her more trying than graceful and answered uncertainly, 'Well, now
I hadn't exactly thought. I need a bit o' help, that's all. 'Course she'd have
to wash the floor and polish it, like, every day. And clean the window and dust
the stock. And when I knowed her a bit she could probably help me with
serving, like. I get proper busy at weekends – and in summer the ice cream
trade brings in a lot o' kids, and you have to have eyes in the back o' your
head or they'll steal the pants off you.'

Mother sniffed at this unseemly mention of underwear, and then nodded.

Match your language to your purpose and audience.

'And what would the salary be?'

I groaned inwardly. I was sure that in a little shop like this one earned wages not a salary.

The beginning of a smile twitched at the woman's lips, but she answered Mother gravely.

'Well, I'd start her on five shillings, and if she was any good I'd raise it.'

Even in those days, five shillings was not much. The woman seemed to realise this, because she added, 'And o' course, she can eat as many sweets as she likes. But no taking any out of the shop.'

I could imagine that this was not as generous as it sounded. After a week of eating too many sweets, the desire for them would be killed and few people would want them any more.

Mother inquired stiffly, 'And how many hours a week would she work for that?'

'Well, I open up at half past seven in the morning to catch the morning trade, you understand. And I close up at nine in the evening.' She paused a moment and then said, 'But I wouldn't need her after about seven o'clock. Me husband's home by then, and he helps me after he's had his tea. And I close Wednesday afternoons, so she'd have the afternoon off after she'd tidied up, like. Me husband helps me Sundays, too, so I wouldn't want her then either.'

I wanted the job so badly that I did not care how many hours I worked, how often I scrubbed the floor. The shop seemed so lovely and warm, after our house, and I sensed that in a rough way the woman would be kind to me. I tried to will the woman to agree to take me.

A little boy burst through the shop door, leaving the bell tinging madly after him. He pushed past us and leaned against the corner of the counter.

'Ah coom for me Dad's ciggies,' he announced, turning a pinched, grubby face up towards the sweetshop owner.

'Have you got the money?'

'Oh, aye. He wants ten Woodbines.' A small hand was unclenched to show four large copper pennies.

The cigarettes were handed over and the pennies dropped into the wooden till.

'Now don't be smoking them yourself,' admonished the woman, with a laugh.

The boy grinned at her and bounced back to the door, his bare feet thudding. As he went through the door, he turned and gestured as if he were smoking.

'Aye, you little gint!' she said.

The interruption had given Mother time to make a rapid calculation. As the woman turned back to her, she said sharply, 'There is a law about how many hours a minor can work – and, incidentally a law about selling cigarettes to minors. I am sure that over sixty hours a week – at less than a penny an hour – are far more hours than are allowed.'

The woman shrugged huffily; her eyes narrowed, giving her a cunning expression.

'I'm sure I don't know about that,' she replied tartly. 'If she doesn't want the job she doesn't have to take it. There's others as will be grateful for it.'

Speak up, don't mumble, speak clearly.

She sniffed, and looked at me disparagingly. 'Anyway, I wouldn't take her. The sores on her face would put the customers off. I got to have a clean looking girl.'

I looked at her appalled, hurt to the quick. In front of our broken piece of mirror, I had carefully squeezed each pimple on my face, so that the acne was temporarily reduced to raised red blotches with a fresh, golden scab on each. I had no make-up to cover the results. But I had hoped that I looked clean.

Mother's face flooded with angry colour. For a moment she looked like Avril in a tantrum. She cast a scornful glance at the shopkeeper, who stared back at her with her chin thrust upwards, quite unabashed.

'Good afternoon,' Mother snapped, as she swung round and opened the street door. The little bell tinkled crossly at being so forcibly disturbed.

'Helen, this way.'

It was an order, and I slouched out through the doorway, closely followed by my wrathful mother.

Avoid a monotonous tone or delivery.

Debates

Procedure
Debates are usually organised in the following way.

1 There are two speakers for the proposal or motion being debated and two against.

2 Those in favour of the motion are the Proposers and those against are the Opposers.

3 There is a chairperson who introduces the topic and calls upon the proposers and opposers to speak. This is done in the following order:
a proposer of the motion,
b opposer of the motion,
c seconder of the motion – who supports the proposer,
d seconder of the opposition.

4 When these four main speakers have had their agreed time, the chairperson asks for questions or other contributions from 'the floor', that is, the audience.

5 Questions and comments should be directed through the chairperson.

6 The chairperson will then ask the proposer and the opposer to sum up briefly.

7 After thanking the speakers, the chairperson will take a vote on the motion which will decide whether it is carried or defeated.

Chairing a debate
The chairperson must be fair and should not express any views on the motion. If you are in the chair, keep control of the debate and insist that all questions and comments are directed through you. Do not allow side arguments to develop.

You must decide whether to ask the main speakers to reply to a particular question straight away or to have them wait until the end to deal with all questions and comments. It is usually better to ask them to note questions and reply in their summing-up.

Set time limits and keep to them although you do not have to cut people off in mid-sentence. Try to involve as many people as possible into the debate. If it seems very one-sided, invite contributions putting the other point of view.

Do not interrupt the other person.

Choice of topics

Choose topics which will allow most people to feel they can express an opinion. Topics related to current news stories are suitable. Social issues are often of general interest, e.g. drunken driving, rising crime rates, homelessness, unemployment, truancy.

The motion should be phrased so that it offers an opportunity for argument, e.g. **Drunken driving is a bad thing** would be a difficult motion to debate as it would be hard to present good arguments against it. But

Drunken drivers should be given long prison sentences *or*
Sales of alcohol should be drastically reduced to curb drunken driving
would provide some scope for debate.

Some samples of motions for debate:

This House considers that motor sports only encourage reckless driving on the roads.
This House believes that competitive sports are socially harmful.
This House believes that it should be illegal for parents to strike their children.
This House believes that the voting age should be reduced to sixteen.
This House believes that women should do more to assert their rights in our society.

Preparation

Main speakers should prepare good notes but avoid reading to the audience. Organise your notes in logical order. Work towards a conclusion.

Try to consider in advance some of the arguments which the other side will use and deal with them in your speech. A series of cards with notes of sections of your speech on them will be useful.

When others are speaking, take notes of any points you wish to comment on later. Good debaters will be able to modify their notes and respond to what others have said in previous speeches.

Performance

1 Speak clearly and avoid slang.

2 Address the audience. You are trying to convince them.

3 Pause when you have made a particular point. Let it sink in.

4 Speak to the audience as though you consider them to be intelligent, reasonable beings who will surely see the sense of your argument.

5 Listen when others are speaking. Show that you have considered their arguments by discussing them and saying why you believe them to be wrong.

Show a lively interest in your topic.

Role play – interviews and telephone conversations

Organise a situation which will allow members of the group to show their oral skills. You may wish to work in pairs. A pair may wish to present a talk to an audience. An Interview is a good example of role play.

The person being interviewed should try to give full answers to the questions, and the person or people asking the questions should try to draw out the interviewee.

Ask open questions rather than closed or leading questions which can only be answered by 'yes' or 'no'.

An open question:
In what sort of surroundings would you like to work?

Closed question:
Would you like to work outside?

Leading question:
You would like to work outside then?

Some other examples of role play used by students are:
a salesperson and customer,
a Manager, salesperson with customer making a complaint,
a parent and child with school report,
telephone conversation – booking holidays, complaining about
dry cleaning, etc.

Remember to listen to the other member or members of the group. Show that you are listening by responding to what they are saying. Encourage other members to contribute by drawing them in and giving them opportunity to join in.

Good speech is more than words.

Aural skills

Good listening is a skill which you can develop and improve. You should learn how to interpret and evaluate what you hear. Listen to the words and also to the tone of voice. Listen for changes in tone and emphasis. Try to pay attention to the way things are said as well as to what is said.

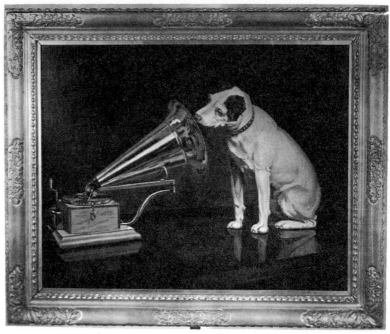

A sense of audience.

Teachers' notes

The passages may be used in the following ways:

1 The students may listen to a passage read aloud once or twice and may then attempt to answer the questions without looking at the passage.

2 They may listen to the passage being read aloud and answer the questions while being able to refer to the printed passage.

3 They may have the passage in front of them during the reading and when they are attempting to answer the questions.

Answers to some questions will depend on the way in which the passages are read. The passages should be read aloud by a competent reader who has prepared them.

Here are some passages which can be read aloud. They are followed by questions which you should attempt to answer in your own words (as much as possible) after you have listened carefully to the readings. Marks for each question are indicated.

Good listening is as important as good speaking.

Passage 1 –
The Great
Ponds

Olumba and his gang floated as silently as they could from one pond to the other. Their eyes were now accustomed to the darkness. They crossed the Pond of Walele and inched their rafts towards the Pond of Wagaba. Olumba placed his men along the neck of water by which they thought the poachers would come.
5 He repeated his instructions to his men and took up his own position.

The Pond of Wagaba was large. No trees grew in it and the branches of surrounding trees tried in vain to form a closely knit roof of foliage above it. There were gaps here and there, and through these the moonlight struck the surface of the pond giving it a leopard-skin effect. Now and then a wild fruit splashed
10 into the pond and a second splash was heard as some fish made for it.

For a long time the night life of the great forest went on undisturbed. The men's eyelids grew heavy and sticky as they tried to blink themselves into alertness. Then suddenly the look-out man came back.

'Men are coming,' he whispered excitedly to Olumba. The latter gave a low
15 whistle much like that of a common jungle bird. He did it three times and heard with satisfaction the gentle rustling of men preparing for action. The poachers came in two rafts. They talked in low tones not because they suspected ambush but because of the overwhelming effect of the ancient forest.

'I feel cold tonight,' one said.
20 'You'll feel warm when you see your trap full of fish,' another replied. Two other men chuckled at the joke.

Olumba guessed he had four men to deal with.

'The Pond of Wagaba can never be impoverished,' one man said. 'I have never seen a pond so full of fish.'
25 'A pity it doesn't belong to Aliakoro,' another said.

'It may one day.'

'How?'

'Eze Okehi, our chief, intends to claim it. He says that Chiolu's claim to it is dubious and that from what his grandfather told him, the pond rightly
30 belongs to us.'

'That will mean a lot of fighting.'

'The pond is worth fighting for isn't it?'

'It certainly is. It will be a great day when we will fish here in daylight without any fears of challenge.'
35 'It should . . .' The man's voice was drowned by a mighty warcry from Olumba's cavernous chest. Amidst splashes the men of Chiolu closed in. The rafts swayed precariously for a moment and were abandoned as dark masses tumbled into the water. There were groans and sighs and the thump thump of heavy blows. Eziho found himself carried shoulder high and dashed into the
40 turbulent water. He got up quickly and grabbed the nearest man. The man's body was slippery and Eziho knew he was holding a comrade. He let go, and looked around. Everyone seemed engaged. Then someone broke loose and ran. He intercepted him and kicked his legs together. The man fell headlong and Eziho fell on him. As he was struggling with his opponent a man ran past
45 closely followed by another. Presently the last man turned back.

'Who is here?' The roaring voice was Olumba's; Eziho could recognize it a mile off.

Listen to the other person before answering.

'Eziho,' came the reply.

'Have you secured your man?'

50 'I am about to. He is still struggling but I . . .' Eziho did not finish. His opponent pushed him off with a savage thrust and got up. The two men came to grips again. Olumba decided to help. He was just in time to prevent Eziho from being dashed violently to the ground. He grabbed the enemy by the waist from behind and pulled him down. Eziho came crashing on them both.

55 Olumba thought that the job was done but the poacher managed to get up and faced them again. Now Olumba was really angry. Who was this that defied his strength?

'Eziho, keep clear,' he shouted as he grabbed the man again. They twisted and turned and pulled until Olumba's anger turned to surprise. His adversary

60 was strong, without a doubt. But he had told Eziho to keep off. He could not call him to help now for shame. He knew he needed more of wits than anger. He let his body go limp and swayed backwards. His opponent followed through. Half-way through his fall he twisted suddenly and had his man on the ground. He pounded the man's head brutally with his fists until he felt him

65 weakening. He loosened a cord round his waist and secured the man's hands.

'I have got him,' Olumba announced.

Look at your audience.

'Well done,' Eziho said.

'He is a very stubborn fellow.'

'As all thieves are.'

70 'I am not a thief,' the prisoner panted.

'Shut up,' Olumba roared. 'You are caught stealing, and you say you are not a thief. You must be the most stupid liar that ever ate fish.'

'I am not a liar,' the captive said.

'People don't trifle with me,' Olumba said and handed out a vicious slap.
75 He raised the man to his feet and pushed him along to join the other prisoners.

'How many prisoners have you?'

'One,' Ikechi said.

'I have two; that makes three. Anyone seriously hurt?'

One man said: 'My left eye is aching, otherwise I am all right.'

80 'All right, let's move. Put the prisoners on the rafts.' Captors and captives boarded the rafts and began to cross the Pond of Wagaba. Olumba was personally in charge of the last man he had fought with.

'By the way, who was the fourth man who escaped?' he asked his prisoner. The man ignored him.

85 'I say, who was the other fellow?' There was still no answer. He slapped the man hard first on the right cheek then on the left.

'It just shows how hardened these thieves are.'

'I repeat we are no thieves,' the prisoner said calmly.

Olumba was beside himself with rage. His hand shot out again but Eziho
90 who was sharing the same raft held his hand.

'Let's wait till daybreak.'

'I have no time to waste. Look, why don't we kill these men right away and declare war on Aliakoro? I have never seen such impudence in my life.'

The men knew that if Olumba got any angrier he would carry out this threat.
95 They did not want this. It was enough to take the prisoners home and ask for large ransoms. Ikechi said, 'You fellows know you are absolutely in our power. Why can't you shut your mouths and think of your troubles?'

'They are all quiet except this stupid fellow here,' Olumba said.

'I am not stupid,' the prisoner said calmly. Olumba was at a loss for words.
100 'Who is this loud-mouthed idiot?' Eziho said.

'I am Wago, the leopard-killer, if you want to know,' the prisoner replied. For a moment a hush fell on the company. Wago the leopard-killer was well known and was a man to be reckoned with. He had three magnificent leopard skins to his credit, a feat unequalled by any man they knew of. His skill in hunt-
105 ing was uncanny. He had on several occasions brought home live antelopes whose bodies bore no traces of any violence or struggles whatsoever. How he caught them no one knew. Tall and sinewy, he was an able wrestler.

Olumba admired brave men. When Wago revealed his identity his anger went down appreciably. Brave men had every right to talk anywhere, he thought.
110 'But Wago, why did you get yourself involved in this disgraceful affair?' Olumba asked.

'What makes it disgraceful?'

'Is it not disgraceful to steal?'

How many um's and er's to the minute?

'How can we steal that which is ours?'

115 'Is this pond yours?'

'Certainly,' Wago said, unperturbed.

'What?' several men shouted simultaneously. The men of Chiolu were surprised and angry.

'And why do you come to fish in the night?' Olumba asked.

120 'To avoid open conflict until our claim has been established beyond doubt.'

'Who gave you this idea?'

'Never mind who did.'

'And you believe we'll give up the pond?'

'Yes, we'll force you to.'

125 Olumba was too full to continue the dialogue. He ordered his men to push on faster. There was no point in arguing with a prisoner who had such ideas.

They floated past the Pond of Wagaba. When they got to the Pond of Walele, Wago pushed Olumba violently to the left and he fell awkwardly into the cold water. Wago dived to the right. By the time Olumba had recovered

130 sufficiently to give orders Wago had disappeared. There was nothing to be done. It was too dark to trace him.

Practice

1 Explain in your own words why the poachers talked in low tones. (2)

2 How does the narrator's pace and tone of voice change when he begins to describe the fight. 'The man's voice was drowned by a mighty warcry . . .' (line 35)? (2)

3 How were Olumba and his men able to tell the difference between friend and foe in the dark? (2)

4 Is there anything in the prisoner's manner or tone of voice which angers Olumba? How does he think the prisoner should speak to him? (3)

5 'I am Wago the leopard-killer, if you want to know.' (line 101) How would you describe the way in which the prisoner says this? (2)

6 What do you think Olumba's feelings are after the prisoner says, 'Yes, we'll force you to'? (line 124) (2)

7 Imagine Wago the leopard-killer's account of the poaching trip when he gets back to his people. Write it in direct speech. (7)

Total (20)

Written English and spoken English are different.

Passage 2 – The Ragged Trousered Philanthropists

Mr Hunter, . . . was executing a kind of strategical movement in the direction of the house where Cross and his mates were working. He kept to one side of the road because by so doing he could not be perceived by those within the house until the instant of his arrival. When he was within about a hundred
5 yards of the gate he dismounted from his bicycle, there being a sharp rise in the road just there, and as he toiled up, pushing the bicycle in front, his breath showing in white clouds in the frosty air, he observed a number of men hanging about. Some of them he knew; they had worked for him at various times, but were now out of a job. There were five men altogether; three of them were
10 standing in a group, the other two stood each by himself, being apparently strangers to each other and the first three. The three men who stood together were nearest to Hunter and as the latter approached, one of them advanced to meet him.

'Good morning, sir.'
15 Hunter replied by an inarticulate grunt, without stopping; the man followed.
'Any chance of a job, sir?'
'Full up,' replied Hunter, still without stopping. The man still followed, like a beggar soliciting charity.
'Be any use calling round in a day or so, sir?'
20 'Don't think so,' Hunter replied. 'Can if you like; but we're full up.'
'Thank you, sir,' said the man, and turned back to his friends.

By this time Hunter was within a few yards of one of the other two men, who also came to speak to him. This man felt there was no hope of getting a job; still, there was no harm in asking. Besides, he was getting desperate.
25 It was over a month now since he had finished up for his last employer. It has been a very slow summer altogether. Sometimes a fortnight for one firm; then perhaps a week doing nothing; then three weeks or a month for another firm, then out again, and so on. And now it was November. Last winter they had got into debt; that was nothing unusual, but owing to the bad summer they
30 had not been able, as in other years, to pay off the debts accumulated in winter. It was doubtful, too,‚ whether they would be able to get credit again this winter. In fact this morning when his wife sent their little girl to the grocer's for some butter the latter had refused to let the child have it without the money. So although he felt it to be hopeless he accosted Hunter.
35 This time Hunter stopped: he was winded by his climb up the hill.
'Good morning, sir.'
Hunter did not return the salutation; he had not the breath to spare, but the man was not hurt; he was used to being treated like that.
'Any chance of a job, sir?'
40 Hunter did not reply at once. He was short of breath and he was thinking of a plan that was ever recurring to his mind, and which he had lately been hankering to put into execution. It seemed to him that the long waited for opportunity had come. Just now Rushton & Co. were almost the only firm in Mugsborough who had any work. There were dozens of good workmen out.
45 Yes, this was the time. If this man agreed he would give him a start. Hunter

Is the room arranged for your best advantage?

knew the man was a good workman, he had worked for Rushton & Co. before. To make room for him old Linden and some other full-price man could be got rid of; it would not be difficult to find some excuse.

'Well,' Hunter said at last in a doubtful, hesitating kind of way, 'I'm afraid
50   not, Newman. We're about full up.'

He ceased speaking and remained waiting for the other to say something more. He did not look at the man, but stooped down, fidgeting with the mechanism of the bicycle as if adjusting it.

'Things have been so bad this summer,' Newman went on. 'I've had rather
55   a rough time of it. I would be very glad of a job even if it was only for a week or so.'

There was a pause. After a while, Hunter raised his eyes to the other's face, but immediately let them fall again.

'Well,' said he, 'I might – perhaps – be able to let you have a day or two.
60   You can come here to this job,' and he nodded his head in the direction of the house where the men were working. 'Tomorrow at seven. Of course you know the figure?' he added as Newman was about to thank him. 'Six and a half.'

Hunter spoke as if the reduction were already an accomplished fact. The
65   man was more likely to agree, if he thought that others were already working at the reduced rate.

Newman was taken by surprise and hesitated. He had never worked under price; indeed, he had sometimes gone hungry rather than do so; but now it seemed that others were doing it. And then he was so awfully hard up. If he
70   refused this job he was not likely to get another in a hurry. He thought of his home and his family. Already they owed five weeks' rent, and last Monday the collector had hinted pretty plainly that the landlord would not wait much longer. Not only that, but if he did not get a job how were they to live? This morning he himself had had no breakfast to speak of, only a cup of tea and
75   some dry bread. These thoughts crowded upon each other in his mind, but still he hesitated. Hunter began to move off.

'Well,' he said, 'if you like to start you can come here at seven in the morning.' Then as Newman still hesitated he added impatiently, 'Are you coming or not?'
80   'Yes, sir,' said Newman.

'All right,' said Hunter, affably. 'I'll tell Crass to have a kit ready for you.'

He nodded in a friendly way to the man, who went off feeling like a criminal.

As Hunter resumed his march, well satisfied with himself, the fifth man, who
85   had been waiting all this time, came to meet him. As he approached, Hunter recognized him as one who had started work for Rushton & Co. early in the summer, but who had left suddenly of his own accord, having taken offence at some bullying remark of Hunter's.

Hunter was glad to see this man. He guessed that the fellow must be very
90   hard pressed to come again and ask for work after what had happened.

'Any chance of a job, sir?'

Hunter appeared to reflect.

Distracting mannerisms distract your audience.

'I believe I have room for one,' he said at length. 'But you're such an uncertain kind of chap. You don't seem to care much whether you work or
95 not. You're too independent, you know; one can't say two words to you but you must needs clear off.'

The man made no answer.

'We can't tolerate that kind of thing, you know,' Hunter added. 'If we were to encourage men of your stamp we should never know where we are.'
100 So saying, Hunter moved away and again proceeded on his journey.

When he arrived within about three yards of the gate he noiselessly laid his machine against the garden fence. The high evergreens that grew inside still concealed him from the observation of anyone who might be looking out of the windows of the house. Then he carefully crept along till he came to the
105 gate post, and bending down, he cautiously peeped round to see if he could detect anyone idling, or talking, or smoking. There was no one in sight except old Jack Linden, who was rubbing down the lobby doors with pumice-stone and water. Hunter noiselessly opened the gate and crept quietly along the grass border of the garden path. His idea was to reach the front door without being
110 seen, so that Linden could not give notice of his approach to those within. In this he succeeded and passed silently into the house. He did not speak to Linden; to do so would have proclaimed his presence to the rest. He crawled stealthily over the house but was disappointed in his quest, for everyone he saw was hard at work. Upstairs he noticed that the door of one of the rooms
115 was closed.

Practice

1 Why did Hunter want to approach the house without being seen? In what way is his effort wasted? (2)

2 What is the difference between the way the first man speaks to Hunter and the way in which Hunter replies? (line 17) (2)

3 Hunter 'was thinking of a plan'. (lines 40–41) What was the plan and why did he think it was a good time to carry it out? (3)

4 Why did Newman feel 'like a criminal'? (lines 82–83) (2)

5 Why was Hunter glad to see the fifth man? (3)

6 Imagine the conversation between Newman and his wife when he goes home to tell her about his job. Write it out in direct speech. (8)

Total (20)

Good listening is as important as good speaking.

Index

Acknowledgements

We are grateful to the following for permission to reproduce copyright material:

The Author, Susannah Amoore for her poem 'At the End of April'; The Bodley Head Ltd on behalf of the Authors, for extracts from *Tales of a Fourth Grade Nothing* by Judy Blume, *Minerva's Stepchild* by Helen Forrester, 'Miss Smith' from *The Day we got Drunk on Cake* by William Trevor; authors' agents for poem 'By St. Thomas Water' by Charles Causley from *Collected Poems* pub. Macmillans; Chatto & Windus Ltd for an extract from *The Bell* by Iris Murdoch; authors' agents for an extract from *They Wait* by Helen Cresswell; authors' agents for an extract from *Boy* by Roald Dahl; Hamish Hamilton Ltd for story 'The Waits' by L.P. Hartley from *The Complete Short Stories of L.P. Hartley*; Headway Publications for articles 'Treasure Trove' by Fenton Bresler from National Westminster Bank *Moneycare* June 1986 'Under 12's and their Money' National Westminster Bank *Moneycare* April, 1986; Heinemann Educational Books Ltd for an extract from *The Great Ponds* by Elechi Amadi (African Writers Series); authors' agents and the Estate of Mrs. Frieda Lawrence Ravagali for extract from 'The Mortal Coil' by D.H. Lawrence in *Pheonix II*; Julia MacRae Books for an extract from *Running Sacred* by Bernard Ashley; authors' agents for an extract from *Science Fiction Omnibus* by Alan E. Nourse; Oxford University Press for an extract from an article in *Oxford Companion to Ships and the Sea* ed. Peter Kemp, 1976; Mrs. Sylvia Secker for an extract from *The Ragged Trousered Philanthropist* by R. Tressell; the Author, Mrs. Sheila Vinson & the Editor *Education and Health* Journal for extract from article in *Education & Health* Vol 3, No 5; authors' agents for an extract from *Black Boy* by Richard Wright, pub. Longman Group UK Ltd (LIB Series).

We have unfortunately, been unable to trace the copyright holder of 'Court Circular' by S. Stokes, and would appreciate any information which would enable us to do so.

We are grateful to the following for permission to reproduce black and white photographs:

Barnaby's Picture Library, page 112; BBC Enterprises, pages 9 right, 36, 200; Camera Press, pages 8 above, 59 (photo: Wilhelm Leuschner), 175 (photo: Gerald Schachmes), 176 (photo: Homer Sykes), 177 above (photo: Ollie Atkins), 177 below (photo: G. Kilkvadze), 183 below (photo: Rolf Mader); © Cannon & Ball 1982, 'Look-in Holiday Special' 1985, Independant TV Publications, pages 104, 105; Carrick James Market Research: Annual Media Income and Spending (AMIS) Survey, 1984, page 143; EMI Records Ltd, page 214; Format, page 92 below (photo: Brenda Prince), 180 (photo: Raissa Page); Sally & Richard Greenhill, pages 91, 92 above left, 92 above right; HAIR magazine, page 110; Headway Publications, page 143; Hutchison Library, page 216; Kobal Collection, page 166; London Features International, pages 8 below (photo: Phil Loftus), 80; Longman Photographic Unit, pages 102; National Film Archive/Stills Library, page 55; Network, page 9 left (photo: Mike Abrahams); Photo Co-op, page

182 (photo: Crispin Hughes); Popperfoto, pages 6 left, 7, 73, 75, 183 above; Press Association, page 6 right (photo: Ron Bell); *Radio Times*, page 111 (photo: Jeremy Grayson); ROSPA, page 141; Sony UK, page 113; Peter de Sousa, Jersey Photographer, page 103; Leslie Stringer & Impact Press Pictures, page 101; Sunderland Polytechnic, page 137; Surrey County Council, page 140; D.C. Thomson & Co. 1987, pages 106, 107, 108; Simon Warner, page 181.

Cover photograph: Trevor Clifford